T0066897

THE GRAVITY OF TRUTH

CHELE MTHEMBU

Order this book online at www.trafford.com
or email orders@trafford.com

Most Trafford titles are also available at major online book retailers.

Printed in the United States of America.

ISBN: 978-1-4907-1280-2 (sc)
ISBN: 978-1-4907-1281-9 (e)

Trafford rev. 09/05/2013

 www.trafford.com

North America & international
toll-free: 1 888 232 4444 (USA & Canada)
fax: 812 355 4082

CONTENTS

THE GATES OF HELL DOES NOT HAVE DOUBLE STANDARDS

". . . . hell is imagined to be in existence somewhere
else after death. But it does not exit after death;
it's actually more alive after birth"

Chele Mthembu

The only time that life can make an entrance through the category of hell, is when a woman gives birth to a child.

The exit mode can therefore be through nothing else but death. When a person gives birth, there is no sin committed on the eyes of humanity. The entrance to this struggle, the struggle being life, makes a human species happy and brings sorrow at the same time. The two can not exist in terms of, one on its own or having acting on a separate space. For their existence, therefore, there should be a closed vacuum; the very same vacuum is indebted in the combination of both the sorrow and happiness of both the man and the woman individually.

About the entrance and the existing mode, let us look on them separately.

Firstly, the entrance, this is birth during a time when a woman give a present in a form of life to the closed vacuum, there should be in this instance, a mutual agreement between her and the man, or one can force the other one to have intimate sex without the concern of the other. In either way, if a woman does nothing to prevent nature from taking its course, nature will provide an entrance to life. In this first look-out, there should be collision and friction taking place between two people, before entrance to the gates of life can be authorized to take place.

Secondly, exiting life, which is death, can either be through the de-generating of the forces that nature used to give the strengths of life, or it can be through the action done by a man species causing friction again, but in a different way than sexual intercourse.

Now during the period of life, man continuing to go through the same mechanism of both collision and friction, that is where a living being can determine the choice to remain on the side of sorrow or happiness, although in some cases the choice does not work as expected. During this period, a living being is more focused on the side of living, bearing in mind the entrance of heaven, so that one can avoid the gates of hell.

One can not decide on avoiding the entrance of this gates, to enter in, is not a choice done by one person concerning his or her life. But this entrance can be decided by the woman who chooses to care, for the fetus period leading to inside the vacuum; the inside of hell is imagined to be in existence somewhere else after death. But it does not exit after death, is actually more alive after birth. The reason we can not realize the hell we are into during our life time, is due to the fact that, the focus has been shifted by the state of fantasizing about heaven.

The avoided arena of hell, and the fantasized arena of heaven, can not be considered operating free from each other. Each one of these two arenas, separated on their own, they do not have the mechanism to sustain life.

If they were to be separated, then it will mean, heaven provide gates only after death, and meaning death only not any form of life suitable for a human being to practice onto it.

Hell is therefore to provide gates to life, and meaning life only, not any gates for death after the exiting of the present life.

The fact that the arena of hell is during the life period is confirmed on:

Isaiah 45:3 when it has been said "and I will give thee the treasure of darkness, and hidden riches of secret places, that thou mayest know that it is I, Jehovah, who call thee by thy name, even the God of Israel."

Further more, if these two arenas were to be separated, although that can only happen through human being imaginative of some sort of a castle in the sky. The separation will translate that, heaven, as the arena of death, can provide room for decomposing, heaven can also be regarded as the storage of the ingredients needed to produce life.

Hence the body of any animal is a tool and the storage arena for what is known as sperms and eggs combining and the end results produce life. Both the sperm and woman eggs, stored separately are also on their state of rest, they are death, hence a woman lead to periods considered as menstruations. The menstruation, in terms of "truth" is the sign of heaven failing to produce life on its own holiness, when hell does not provide its gates for entrance, to the other side of hidden richness of secret places and treasures of darkness. Therefore what heaven hold is not a complete life, but only the state of rest, which is to be utilized at a given point taking place when both heaven and hell state of arenas, execute their unlike poles of forces of attraction, will there be life.

The arena of hell, on its own is the state of motion, and the mind activities. These simply means that whenever the body makes any kind of motion against friction, or the mind and heart having generated either feelings of excitement or sorrow, in sickness, richness and health, it is the arena of hell. And this arena can not go beyond any means of its due restrictions.

At the time when the body is doing whatever it takes to guard its healthy state against sickness and sorrow, it is when the arena of hell is busy guarding the well being of heaven. Remember I said heaven is the state of rest, when destruction take place, heaven have no means to protect itself, but rely on the protection of the state capable of response, the state of motion, and that is the arena of hell. That is way only after the force of motion respond provided by the arena considered to be of the dark side, can destabilization of the state of rest take place.

After death both heaven and hell can not produce life of the same species as the death one. That is due to decomposing taking place for another life, which is for minerals to be taken-up by both soil and plants. But the two can not be categorized to be part taking in the process of practicing some sort of any kind of entrance to either the gate of hell or the heaven one. Hence if you get; flesh separated from its soul, neither one of the two can be punishable; the fact being that, they are out of the closed system. The super power creator did not go beyond the means of flesh and soul to be independently functioning. They can therefore only be punishable, if they are dependable to each other in a close vacuum. You are done with your service to God while you are still alive, after that, God of Israel has no use for you, as the death has no meaning to the present functioning of Israel as part of the world chosen for "the treasure of darkness, and hidden riches of secret places".

A quote from the bible, Jeremiah 51:48-49 (Then heaven and the earth, and all that is therein, shall sing for joy over Babylon; for the destroyer shall come onto her from the north, said Jehovah. As Babylon has caused the slain of Israel to fall, so at Babylon shall fall the slain of all the land" end quote.

This quote translate that, the punishment of what you do in the world will come back and hunt you while you are onto the world, it will then end onto the world, not to be carried to the other world that doesn't have the brain to sustain differences.

THE NATURE OF LIFE, UNDER NEATH THE STATUS OF SELFISHNESS

'People, who spent too much time in the session of regretting, are those who are brainwashed deeply by the fact that wrong is a sin. Wrongs practice drives right, and above all, right practice, also drives wrongs'

Chele Mthembu

Selfless, it is a quality within a human being; it has a purpose for inclusion of others and their needs. As much as it has been valued, it is said that it is a Godly value to have. I can not negate that. My take is on its opposite meaning, the nature of life, underneath the status of the so called selfishness.

The center in which everything in life has been formulated from, it is mostly the one centre that is either pulled by the attraction force or pushed by the repelling one. This is called the principle of the self-centered. It is the center about you.

The power of this principle is made-up and is driven-up by the force of self esteem, the interest that makes you alive, and the spirit giving you the ability to respond. The principle of self centered rules the principles of success. Both of this principles, self-centered and success are the two principles power-up forcefully by the principle of selfishness.

Under taking the principles of selfishness, requires one to have a high self esteem. People in this category of life style, walk with their head-up, with their chin well positioned and their nose also well pointed, to the direction in which the wind containing the smell of the greener pasture comes from. Don't forget that this is the center in which a series of small and big events are connected, and the person in the middle of those events to over see that the chain goes on, to the point of new invention, is you.

For starters let me make the clarification of one thing first here, it is absolutely not a bad things for one to be selfish.

It does not even carry the weight of being a sinner. Selfishness it is just a principle that is well practice by those who are the rulers of the small world of their own; this is the world about building a center to over see your own interest and explore them accordingly.

The best thing about people who are self centered is that, they don't believe in being driven by passion to make things happen. Their center is about getting thing done without having to leave them to chance. Their center is all about attraction and repelling force. Whether there is passion presence on their feelings or not, they push things to the point in which they need to be pushed. They attract opportunities to their center, taking the present moment as the determining factor of success.

What makes a selfish person different? What makes them accumulate the principle of success at all times? The answer is that, selfishness principle has no room for passion. Selfishness has an allergic feeling to what is known as passion. The two principles can not go hand to hand. Passion is the principle that is based on the right feeling, the right time and the right career for its domination to take place. This is what makes selfishness to be allergic to passion.

The power of being selfishness does not have the waiting period, as much as the passion status has for the right time, the presence work just fine for selfishness. It is not career connected, but, it is a career at its own center.

With the combination of being responsible, the center of selfish has only one goal to attain, it is about attaining the ability to respond. Not just any responding ability but the most specialized one. In any list of top performers, it can be in the sporting code, a corporate world or the entertainment industries, people who have their names appearing there, are the ones that took the advantage of learning the art of specialized responding ability, powered by being selfish giant reactor.

You are having your feet firmly on the ground and you are in possession of the attitude of the champion. Attitude of the world heavy world champion is what you are in a possession of it within you. You saw a weakness in your opponent and you know that it is going to work for your own advantage.

Getting your feet firmly and putting all your weight behind your shoulders, is what you need to be doing. If ever there is a bruising on the eye, it is the best thing for the other fighter to make a beating as much as he can on that eye. Getting that eye more injured put you in the right sport of getting the fight to be shorter than it has to be. It is a fact not to be ignored or left out. Failure to make more beating on the injured side may result in the fight being taken from you, with a technical nock-out. This is the stage one, powered by selfishness quality. This is one stage that is very crucial in the lifestyle of those who are governed, by the power of fishing at their own. They do believe that for things to happen one need to be self involved, for goals to be achieved in the exact time, in the manner in which they will prefer, they've got to be mentally involved, emotionally involved, and above all physically involved.

Stage two, the state of selfishness, the state of self involvement for fishing, is the formulation and construction of foundation.

It happens to be, the central room, the control room, for your life. It is the executing stage whereby the feeling of fear doesn't have any control over a person, failure is not an option.

Selfish practice is done by the people who are excellent in exploring all the possibilities. Selfish people are the heavy weight that rules the world of finance.

As heavy weight as they are, they don't leave things to chance, fear of consequence and circumstances, has no influence in executing their action. They act when the world says they can't be because it will be a sin. They act even though the situation seems to be hopeless.

When the situation, seems to be having a side in which is considered to be conducive, taking advantage of that small crack visible on the eye sight, is the benefiting factor which is exactly what they have to go for.

Results may either becoming with some consequences or not, but after roll, in both ways, it is the name of the game for personally becoming involved in fishing. After taking advantage of whatever they where fishing for, they will take two steps backwards in the process allowing the present created situation to work for them. This is simply done by playing and manipulating the minds of others whom are involved in the very same process.

People practicing the principle of selfishness; knows that, the circumstance coming with the stigma of being labeled on such category is nothing but just the mindset of the human being. To change these two forces that occupy the larger potion of the mind; one needs to have self modification, know how to execute game rule, to them any time is, right time, and the right place with the right people. Executing the action to implement an idea makes the difference of whether you remain poor, out of touch with love, stay thinking in the walls of the box or getting total freedom.

Thinking in the manner that benefits you, in both financial and good health is the only kind of thinking that is preferred, and it was meant to be like that from the beginning. The kind of thinking that were masterminded by the master of brainwasher and his teachings, is no longer an option simply because it is the fake of what we truly stands for.

- Religious taught us to love and not to practice the act of selfishness.
- Taught us that money is the roots of all evil.
- It went on teaching us that we need to give in order to receive.
- And put the needs of others before our needs.

The rules of the game have to be changed in here. Everything has to be reworked with the aim of taking our minds back to the original state. The state it was before, the master piece meant for self power. But now for majority, just analyze it presently; it is brainwashed, emotional boxed thinking tool, conditioned for benefiting others.

Hence self power has been turned to be the cash generating factor, for the master of conditioner.

The former South African president Thabo Mbeki said, from his speech, 'the Historical Injustice '. I quote:

a. "We are producers of wealth;
b. We produce this wealth for our own benefit to be appropriated by us the producers;

c. The aim of this production shall be the satisfaction, at an increasing level, of the material and spiritual needs of the people;

d. We shall also order the rest of the society and social activity, in education and culture in the legal sphere, on military questions, in our international relations, et cetera, to conform to these goal" end of quote.

The rules of the game based on the power governing the principle of selfishness state that "in other to make it in the world of the material driven by money, receive first and multiply. Appreciates and be satisfied by what you have produced. Then you can only give away after multiplication of what you have received". This is the principle that God himself gave to a man to practice, when he said "live by what you have sweat for."

The person who is rich is the one who truly love himself. Put his needs first and multiply what he has, and only then, can he be able to give what his world of self centered have produced. Being poor in financial matters and love because one is thinking that it is the will of God, for you thinking of other before yourself rob you the true will of God to be happy through enjoying what is rightful your.

There is no legacy of regret on the hearts and the mind of those people whom are thinking out of the box. They took a risk of remaining single; they took a risk of collecting different material with the value of money attached to it. They have traveled around the world. They met people, they made some impact on those people one way or the other, and then they left to the other direction. They made impact on others as they please. Telling things the way they are, it's what works really best for them. Either you are getting hurt of what they are saying or, whatever the impact their words have on you has nothing to do with them.

To avoid the legacy of regret they are always in the look out for the protection of their territories, by doing what need to be done no matter the consequences. This is the act that has nothing to do with intentionally hurting others or undermining them in any way; it's just the principle of avoiding the future health hazards that comes with the regrets of, why I did such a thing? Why didn't I do things differently? Only if I had done thing differently, things could have been otherwise.

- Be selfish about your health.
- Be selfish about your money.
- Time is a valuable thing, be selfish about how you spent it. If ever you give it for the benefit of others let it be on your terms, not on the terms based on the teaching specified by the society's expectations.
- Don't let people take advantage of your talent, it is a God given product to you, so why not,

capitalize on in by making sure that others are paying for it.

The act of self engaged in fishing, has no time for fools who have no time to stand their grounds, by wanting to go back from where they are, to the previous life. The previous experience is the legacy that mostly they turn to capitalize on. Either it is a bad or good experience they make the best out of it.

People, who spent too much time in the session of regretting, are those who are brainwashed deeply by the fact that wrong is a sin. Wrongs practice drives right, and above all, right practice, also drives wrongs.

Those who are telling us that we should practice right only, it is the same as they can teach us that light is better and darkness is not. Light and darkness work the same for the planet earth. The very same people teaching us to be, only on the right path exposed to the light, are the masters of people exploration.

They have discovered the secret weapons of the darkness. Selfish is the art of hunting, when you are busy practicing on the path you have been channeled to follow, by being only the spectator of life, spectators of the great hunters, they are capitalizing on the other hand the effort invested in channeling you. When they are done with you, to be such a life spectator, they are living life according to the true principles of living, and that is to be the self engaged hunter, producing wealth and be satisfied by it as Thabo Mbeki has said. This is the art of self-interest, powered mainly by its device selfish center according to my extended version of reasoning at its best.

But let's go on with this to see how those who are at your surrounding will end-up benefiting.

The world is ruled by capitalism, hence a capitalist what he did was to interrupt our thought, in order for us not to take our interest before hand, he then found a better way by channeling us in the direction which lead back-wards, from the one taking us the ordinary people, to practicing away from the 'Goddess perfection' rather than within. He then removed our minds from getting our self center well established and transformed.

The transformation of the mind is the one factor that have what it take to go kick, these closed doors that the real treasure of life is hidden behind them. The point of becoming old, will at some stage reach you. So the time to take advantage of hunting to prepare for the old age necessities is now. Most of the blacks are the victims of being channeled to one way, that has no turning point, and it has killed the preparation and the richness of their legacy.

The secret of life is locked somewhere, transformation of the mind, with mental passion, allows you to take a kick and open those locked doors. If your kick doesn't do enough, then take a grinder, and make the damage to that door. Damage it in such a way that it will not be able to closed again. This is not the act of using a violence, it is a God given right to have that sacred available for us, for the well being of our true happiness which has rich legacy.

What exactly inspired a fish to make one choice and stick by that choice, was the act of selfishness. Frogs choose to live both in the water and dry grounds. A fish only choose water. Crocodiles choice both water and land. But a fish only stayed on with the option of water. The question is then why water rather than dry ground was suitable for this kind of an animal.

This was influenced by the behavior act of selfness. When other animals including a human being, make the efforts of dealing with the wind, heavy rains and any heat directly in the dry ground, the fish was satisfied with the fact of dealing with this natural factor indirectly on its own terms and conditions.

A fish is inspired by going up against the waves created by the wind and heavy rains. When the results of these natural factors bother those who are on the dry ground, for a fish it is a privilege on its life. Staying dry of motivation, staying dry of the inspiration is the most likely choice we turn to choose, even though it is not necessary.

Pride keeps us away from the things that matters the most in life. We give too much attention on building the right words to come out of other people's mouth, about what they have to say concerning who we are. People's words can turn to make you dry of inspiration. You've got to go head-on with whatever others are throwing on you, like a fish going head-on with the wave of the sea. You've got to stay motivated as if you are a fish sailing slowly, in the river where the weather is calm, in the shinny summer day.

Every day when you got out of a bedroom, do find something to keep you motivated for the rest of the day. Maybe you are HIV, diabetes or any life threatening disease; it won't do you any good to feel sorry on how you've got the disease. Find a reason to be motivated by small things like mental exercising and take the problem in your system as if, it is one of the made-up strength, let the disease or any kind of life challenges be the "extra systemic power generated by the mental" to a better healthy, this will eventually reverse the rate in which your body is getting weak. The positively you feel make's the difference to one's health.

It takes the feelings of getting healed to be completely healed. The marriage may be having some troubles, be inspired by the fact that your partner is in need of something special that need your attention, for that matter, at the present moment make efforts that will come-up with a turning point, challenge that will keep you motivated for the rest of the day. One inspiration has to lead to the other. Touch is one of the greatest medicines. How about massaging her or him before bed time? That can make the one effort leading to the best changed attitude towards each other. For the rest of the day you mind won't be occupied by the troubles you'll be facing at home, but by the thought of making the best out of troubled situation.

It is the thought of how things can be changed, that make the journey of getting to the other side of troubled situation to be more exciting, than giving one stress.

Think of what will the morning after the troubled situation be like? These are the question that can keep you wet of inspiration for the rest of the day, as much as the fish can manage to stay wet for its entire life, dryness kills it. Choosing to be dry for the sake of others will also kill you.

This does have the power to take your work performance to the upper level, simply because you are wet of motivation for that singled point in life. it is not the end results that matter so much in life, but the small steps and efforts taken and putted together one day at a time that make the significance in one's life. After roll it is this small pieces glued together that make the end results. Be motivated and always find the reason to stay wet of inspiration. Deal with life indirectly as much as fish dealing with external force of nature in the indirect manner. The options is basically your.

For the most well operating network of capable technological device like the computer and other sources of communication, there must be a certain source that connects them together.

The best capable server produces the best operating network. Your self centered need to be functioning like a server. Your door has to be open for those who will be turning for help from you.

Due to the ability to respond possessed by the selfish practicing people, they must have the helping hand available for the needy ones. The main principle of selfishness is based on helping yourself first, this is the principle of "first thing first, to be done" that is one thing no man should never over look or ignore. Help yourself as much as you can before thinking of giving for benefits to others, that will prevents the circumstances leading to your self centered world getting dry. It is how much that you have gathered that determine how much power you got to serve others, based on your terms of whether you are interested on giving or not.

It is not a sin to leave all you've worked for in the hands of your loved ones only.

The difference between the poor and the rich is the strategy applied above the average that mostly makes the cut. And it is not entirely centralized in the fact of being a hard worker. Above average kind of thinking produces the results that are above average, which are the ones that are preferred by the richest. Below average kind of thinking produces normal results under average which make an ordinary person satisfied.

The practice of selfishness was engineered to be an immoral practice with the aim of taking advantage of those whom ended up having felt for this trap. Refuse the legacy of being taken advantage off by others putting you in the boxed mind. Have your mind stretched, with your horizons well positioned, with different angles of your life connected like a technological devices to one operating server. Let this be your ambitious powered by the principle of fishing on your own self strategic terms.

For your life to receive transition, the only one person having the right set of choices for such process is you. Therefore, how about you do yourself a favor, subscribe to 'passion of the mind' to make a transition of your mind from the box kind of thinking mind, to the transformed kind of thinking mind that is not conditioned and has what it takes to self engage in fishing for its destiny.

DETAILED STRATEGIC THINKING

Bad, means the combination of one having
the quality, experience and expertise of being
"best achiever and developer".

Chele Mthembu

In every aspect of life, for something to be done, no matter what it is, the best laid out plan is needed, this is an old known practice.

It has to be the best detailed one, from the picture of the "end" backwards to the starting point. You know, a person who operates in this kind of focused mind, the mind which is "detailed strategic thinking" he has an idea, attainable goal and a plan of action that can be broken into a series of successful achievement.

Detailed strategic thinking is all about the ability to "break up the impossible situation to be simply possible ones". The method that I'm presenting here is the one which is mostly practiced by the minority all around the world. The reason being, they have learned and had the opportunity at an early age to discover the importance, the logic and the art of living life, from the end, backwards to the starting point.

Let us make a reference to the wild animals, the Lion. The Lion without any contradiction is the most dominating animal, the greatest animal that is considered to be king of the jungle.

- What makes the Lion such a domination animal?
- What makes it, a king of the jungle among other wild animals?

For starters, go through the real meaning of the four, alphabetical letters that are found on the name of this wild animal, king of the jungle, the Lion.

L—Stand for learning;
I—Stand for intelligence;
O—Stand for organizing;
N—Stand for nature.

From the day of birth, a young Lion is practically born as a king of the jungle. Either way, it does not matter at all, whether it is a male or a female. The Lion was born a king; it was given the quality and the leadership skill to dominate as the king of the jungle.

Making the comparison; of this scenario to a human being. We are born with a hand in a form of a fist. We are born with the right to have everything in this world, for the world to be controlled by our hands and mind. This wild animal, the Lion, may be born to be the king of the jungle, and it's limited to dominate to that field only. But we the human being, we were born beyond the limit of governing to one field only. Our destiny has been determined to govern right from the moment of birth. So why are we mostly controlled by the situations? Where this mentality of things being impossible does comes from?

Where have we lost our birth right, which is to govern the world beyond the limit, and see the impossible as being possible?

Let's go back and explore the behavior, quality and leadership of the Lion, as king of the beast, as its birth right enables it, it has been said that,

"Lion hunt in teams to bring down large animals such as the buffalo in the down-wards picture. They approach their prey stealthily, fanning out to cut off escape routes, until they are within about 30 m (100 ft). At this point the hunters charge. A successful charge— about one in four—ends when one lioness bites the downed animal on the throat or muzzle, suffocating it. Males rarely participate in the hunt, but their size enables them to muscle into the feeding circle".

As we have said "N" in the name Lion stands for nature or naturally. This quality is one of the strongest in the Lion's life.

- It is, its nature to stork and kill its pry in a smartly way, without hard working.
- By just roaring, it makes its natural domination to be felt.
- It is its nature to be the best. It is its birth right to be the greatest.
- Naturally no matter how small or young it is, its presence makes other big animal to run with their tail between their legs.

But as wild as the Lion is, it also knows that in order to do things near perfection, you needs to take into consideration that, in every aspect of life, first thing has to be done first. It is therefore best for one to practice the principle of first thing first.

'L" stands for learning, but a Lion was not born to learn, it was born to lead the jungle. But apart from that, as a king, it believes in doing things near perfection.

That is why it follows other big Lion to learn the greatest skill of hunting and killing smartly although it was born with such skills. Born a king and a leader, but it practiced the principles of first thing first, which is to learn from those who know the rules of the game and how to get them twisted so that they can work in you advantage. Life has too much rules, sometimes it is better to know when to ignore them or just to bend them a little, or for good.

The bad thing about these rules is that they are the reasons that fear is created, which affects our success and happiness, and hide such good reflection of ourselves deeper in our subconscious.

Majority of us human being had no time to learn things near perfection. To do things near perfection, one has to go all the way to break the impossible situation to be simply possible, without delegating attention to fear of the out come.

For that to be accomplished, the following has to be done.

1. Transfusion:

The flow of knowledge, finance, love and protection has to be from the point of high concentration (The rich people) to the point of low concentration (The needy one.) If you are poor, take as much as you can, from what may be presenting your way. The rich man has also applied the very same methods, why can't you use it too? If you don't, be prepared to be the slave of the observers with the intention to take for themselves.

2. Enabling environment:

Expand your capacity for the richness, including knowledge, finance, protection and love, to flow smoothly to your enabled environment powered by the law of transfusion. Knowledge comes mostly when you are at the wrong place or things not going you way, it by this time that you need to learn as much as you can about the loose ends and record them accordingly. When you are faced with tough life battles, it is where you capacity is more suitable for receiving more. Simply meaning, troubles prepares you for success.

3. Accessibility:

The time you put in, the positive attitude and the 'I can, kind of mind', becoming the fuel that drive one to the point of getting success at the end of the journey of trial and errors. Each error needs to be one building block to attaining break-through. Take them as a fortune to have one in you life.

4. Moisture:

Never let your environment dry, always have it moist with patience, driven by the law of transfusion. What others knows, what you have learned from them, needs your development. Practice to be a developer of ideas, for new one to keep you entertained.

5. Strengthen:

The kind of leap of faith exercised in here is the one in which your guts feelings are getting stretched, to take you from that point of the attitude that says "I can make it happen" and really make it possible. Form the mental picture of what you want and remain calm to save you strengths under difficulties troubling you.

6. Pressure:

Circumstances is the name of the game when coming to the art of turning things from the feeling of being impossible to the feeling of possibility, that is way, one has to act in the road of realistically manner. Don't let pressure to stretch your horizon, unless you are well equipped with the right tool to get the job done. The right tools are mostly represented by knowledge as the leading factor, and the rest comes secondly. You can have as much as you can, as long as you knowledge is backed-up by the "I can attitude" and not necessarily limited by the circumstances.

7. Impossibilities:

The unseen are made visible before the plan is even executed. In the mind it should be appearing like a done deal.

8. Repetition:

Here the process of whatever that is working as the greatest formula in you life, is just getting repeated to fold up the results for best output expected.

9. Interrupting:

After pressurizing and the environment is considered well moistured, to the level in which the impossibilities are made possible, meaning you have attained you goal, then, the environment is once again interrupted, with the aim of creating the newly favored enabling one.

10. Turning-point:

After each accessibility of transfusion in which desired out-put has been reached, there must be a turning point taking place. A new pressure with stretching mechanism is then enabled by the turning point to the direction towards what we live for, our destiny. Do not practice in one field only, life does not operate like that, the importance of a turning point is basically to spread you wings. Each direction explored should produce another experience of its own.

The process in witch Osmosis take place state that's, diffusion take place, from the place of high concentration to the place of low concentration. Having an idea converted to a vision with the same impossibilities due to lack of information and finance requires the following, which is also from the place of high concentration to the dry one by the pulling force of the desire to be better.

- This is how it works, its all getting started with the enabling environment. It is the step of two different state of environment. The first one is wet and rich of information; finance and analytical kind of strategizing. The second one is just dry; with the highest capacity of enabling the new look for its self; that is the new age of possibilities. You need to look at things like that.
- There has to be some of the mechanism available for accessibility of transfusion to be enabled. Once your environment is well moist, get it stretched, whatever the kind of detailed strategies you may come across from your achieves, let them be your weapon to the future. Invest in yourself and let others also to invest in you. But take your cut with interest, if not favors.
- Once the first step is accomplished, always the system has to be interrupted. Believe me; involving new people in this interruption can be more benefiting than dealing with the same

people over and over, the interruption enables the turning point to have bigger capacity for the next process to take place with clear focus and the same vision, which the first step was accomplished with.

Man and women, have failed in many occasions to kill the problem from its roots so that, other parts of the problem won't require lot of work to complete in taking care off situations. A person first mistake results in a failure to cut off escape routes of what is troubling him

To be the greatest, a Lion keeps the company of the greatest. But we human just keep any company for the sake of belonging to a certain group. We hide behind it like a terrified girl fearing the horror which is not even close from happening. We have the guts to buck aloud while we are in such groups like a dog bucking with sharp and strong teeth, but without the guts to make a bite.

The intelligence of the Lion, which is represented by the "I" letter on its name; it comes only into the picture, when the Lion is in the stage of re-calling what its nature is all about. The recalling processes are done after the learning process. Once the recalling state of mind has been done and completed, then fallows the organizing skills. These are the skills of being organized, being organized comes from the process of learning the art of detailed strategic thinking, detailed strategic thinking which is the only factor that qualifies you to be intelligent.

Woman need not to have a man in her side to be intelligent deal maker in the survival of the family, as much as the female Lion take the lead in hunting, a woman can make it too on the role of taking any kind of organization or family to a new height she prefers to reach.

'O' which is for the organizing skills. It is all about timing. When stocking it's pray the Lion know when to attach and the art of attacking smartly, they approach their prey stealthily, fanning out to cut off escape routes, until they are within about 30 m (100 ft). At this point the hunters charge. When hunting, its mission is to stock and kill, only the killing determine the success of its mission nothing else.

The question that one may ask here is that, why then can't we measure up to this wild animal, since we were born without any limits, we were born beyond the measure that makes or determines what is known as the limitation. The difference here is that the wild animal took some time to delay process of being the king of the beast in order for it to move fast in the future. Moving slowly at early age comes with some advantages attached to it.

It is wise for us to take advantage of every spot we find our self in, but the fact of the matter remains, you need to be ready for a road to destiny. Even though you were born ready, with your destiny already determined, the recalling process through learning is essential. The road to destiny is full of doubt and the thought of things being impossible; in order to make the break through to attain goals near perfection, there is an art to mastered first.

What is meant by doing thing near perfection? And what is the art to be master first?).

The young Lion was born with the skill and the right to be the king, but it has delayed that right by first studying the behavior of other older hunting Lions and also other animals in general, that was the art of first thing first kind of mindset. Although it has learned the behavior of other animals, it did not learn the hunting skill of a Tiger or any other predators, and it did not want to take any character of such predators. It only leaned those that it will have them against it's prays.

The kingdom was its destiny. Once it felt the readiness after it has recalled its intelligence and the capability to be organized. It did not waste any second to claim what the nature had given to it during birth, which is the right to govern as the king, the right to be feared, the right to dominate in the jungle. The jungle being the place in which only the one's with the best survival skills has the chance to make it day-in and day-out.

The fact that a human being fails to be like the wild animal is based on the time delaying strategy. In charge at an early age is not a wise move. It makes you focus on single angle, which in turn resulting in missing the picture of becoming broad minded. Take time to learn from the expert, gather your intelligence first.

Be organized first, and when you know that you are ready to lead, then you can go back to the day you where born and claim your right to govern life without any limit.

- It is the guts feeling that you have learned from an early age that will defiantly determine how focused you will stay on you road to destiny.
- It is the same guts that will give you the courage, to make the breakthrough in most fearful situation, the break through after the relationship that didn't work on our favor. The break through to successful life that is not under the bondage of unnecessary rules that are man made.
- Governing life without the expectation of others requires detailed strategic thinking. To be the best strategic thinker, learn to live life from the backward to the starting point. The starting point is where you destiny lay.

I remember some time ago while I was still in primary grade, I did not have the guts to stand in front of other children to make a presentation.

By the time I was born it was my destiny to do presentations for a living, it was there for a must for me to nature my guts to be a highly self-esteemed man, with the courage to make cash out of words. Which is exactly what I have done; in a process that took a certain period.

The fact that I was shy by that time helped me to delay the process so that I can first watch what other are doing and how they are doing it. How different can I be from them? That was based on the matter of being the speaker of his own kind, when coming to the fact of detailed strategic thinking. Finally I went back to the day that I was born to claim my right, my destiny, my survival formulae and method of earning a living.

Today I'm a public speaker with the guts to take necessary risks.

Today I'm a man who is living his destiny. I'm' on the road to greatness, it is a biter road, but I am getting there day-in and day-out, bit by bit.

What is it that you are yesterday?

What is it that you will be today?

What is it that you will be tomorrow?

Yesterday determine today, today determine tomorrow, the future is entirely based on the days before. The right thing you did on the past, the wrong thing you did on the past. All of those things form the bigger picture. Good things combined with the bad things you did make a complete product, which is you. You are the bad things you have engaged on from your teenager's age to the stage of adulthood. Bad, means the combination of one having the quality, experience and expertise of being "best achiever and developer".

It is the responsibility of the man to see to it that his children's are well equipped with the right tools and methods of survivals. The different method of survival is the kind of method not determined by the expectation of others, but determined by the individual taking into consideration the maturity level for his actions, due to the art of first thing first.

If a person is a gay, why should; his sexual activity be questioned by us and having it subjected to be a wrong practice. If it is that practice that makes the person to reach the feeling of ultimate pleasure in sexual activity, then let it be their practice, who the hell on earth are we to question the creation of God, whereas we fail to be faithful to those we married too.

Give the child the right skill of how to catch a fish; once you have done your part, it is up to the child to go back to the day he was born to claim his birth right, the right to live life beyond the limitation, the right to govern. If it is a girl and she chooses to be a sex worker, then why not? That could be the field that she was born to rule.

The sex world is her field of expertise, let her govern that field without having to condemn her practice, it is her birth right any-way to lead and take control on the entertainment using the art nature as much as the female Lion take the lead in its field of hunting. Whether you name her prostitute or a sex worker, it matters not. The fact of the matter is that, she has claimed her right to be on the entertainment industry. It is a method of earning a living whether we like it or not. Ignoring and bending the rules here is a factor that she will practice. What really surprising here is that, those who are not sex workers but clients, also are engaged on helping her to bend such rules making prostitution illegal and, as a sinful practice.

The wise king in the bible once had the wisdom from God, and he made a choice to have hundreds of affairs with deferent women that even God did not approve of them. But it is God that gave him that wisdom and he used it accordingly to uphold peace. Same applies, God gave the women the beauty and the different method of entertaining. If the women choose to earn a living with that beauty in any way, let it be.

An organization trading as a service provider makes a capital investment, time effort and at the end it charges according to the investments and the service provided to the customer. Such organization just makes the advertisement of their service and how best they are when coming to completing the project they under take. It is the customer that makes the consultation at the end of the day. They are prepared to seal a deal to pay for the charges coming with that service provided.

A sex worker makes her beauty to be noticed by investing capital and time effort to her career, just like big organization are strategizing. The sex worker has to learn all the technique that is required in her field of duty. Which involve the art of communicating, with a client, isn't that one of the sales representative skills? The manner in which she has to massage her client has to be different form the massages the clients get from home.

As much as detailed strategic thinkers they are, this women, they have invested their time on reading peoples like they read a novel which its ending can be predictable.

They mostly mastered the art of reading people through two factors; they read their client through the facial expression, and the tone of their voice. It is by this expertise that one need to respect sex workers.

- They are the queens in the art of entertainment. Their body has been made priceless; it is therefore, necessity in that case for them to have the value of money attached, on whatever the service or work provide through their state of art received as a blessing.
- They are the smart workers that have what it takes to convert nature into a method of surviving.
- Just like Solomon was up holding the peace through affairs, they are practicing the same

thing by keeping the soul of the man entertained and happy.

- They are as equal with the organization that trade-in as the service provider. It is the client that makes the consultation and put the offer on the table to pay for the service to be provided.

Look man, this is the main reason that Jesus did not pass any judgment to the lady found on the prostituting practice, Jesus knew that we have all prostituted many times, and it is not a sin to appreciate what God have created. It does no good for man, not enjoying what have been specifically made for him to enjoy to the fullest, whereas, he only live once in this world.

The guts feeling to live their lives without the bondage of the expectation of others, makes them well qualified to be, categorized as people who reject to be brain washed, in order to believe in what is not their course in life. The society then labels and shames them simply because they have not been conditioned as expected by the master of conditioner. They have therefore past the test of maintaining their true identity. Leave them alone; find your own worth rather than spending your short life time make the unauthorized judgments. They are having a life, rather than persecute them, how about mastering the courage to reject the teachings that have conditioned a man.

TEN COMMANDMENTS FOR THE MOVEMENT OF PASSION

"How I behave, is the combination product of,
the reasoning and action model I have
commanded in myself identification"

Chele Mthembu

Principles as having been stated from the dictionary, as the basic truth, general law that is used as the basis of reasoning, guide-line to action, guide-line to behavior.

a. How you reason, guide how you take actions;
b. how you take actions, then guides and generate your behavior pattern;
c. how you behave, is then the combination product of, the reasoning and action model one have commanded in self identification.

It has to do with ten categories or laws of principles, such categories are as follows:

1. Purpose
2. Re-bounce
3. Implementation on self concept
4. Nail
5. Culture
6. Identity
7. Power
8. Leaders of circumstances
9. Engage
10. Series

Self classification is influenced by the combination of the above listed principles. The capacity you advance in each of them, provide the escape from struggling to maintain the chain of events leading to mental freedom for;

- Clearly identified purpose,
- Clearly culture identified.

Western culture need not to be the culture that gives you identity. African culture need not to be the practice that gives you the real picture of who you really are. Your culture starts right at an early age, by the time you start identifying and step by step, one category of principles at a time practiced and perfected through your belief.

1. PURPOSE

"Faith, purposely, it was not designed so that we can trust that God will help us out on our set of missions"

Chele Mthembu

In its real definition, it is the intention of a person willingness to become a brand which is driven and influence-by, a set of guidelines weighing through one's appearance, and the power of spoken words when negotiating your way out of unappreciated situation leading to the 'enabled environment'.

Personal self generated force, it was specifically made by God himself, so that, it can be able to take you through whatever that life may take you on with. Challenge you get out of life, are there for you to be tested in order to find out what you've got to offer. It is to find-out how great you can stand your grounds. Can you put your money where your mouth is?

Purpose is structured with the most powerful factor which is the spiritual; or rather say faith as it is well known. Faiths, is the one and above all, mother of all other categories that made-up what is being referred to as principles.

When ever the preachers are teaching us about the word of God, they turn to be having limiting the power of faith. According to them, those whom refer to themselves as the man serving almighty, faith in God is about doing things while waiting for God to perform his miracles on you. They say that you have to do you part and God will complete the process.

The human being was not created incomplete; the process was completed both in our inner image and outer image.

- The inner image is formed by our brains and hearts.
- The outer image is formed by our physical image.

Faith, purposely, it was not designed so that we can trust that God will help us out on our set of missions, in order to reach our target in life. Faith was made so that we can have complete trust that we can create life.

The multiplication does not have the limit to either right or wrong, both of this practice, was given the go ahead to capacitate onto multiply. God gave us that rights when he said go and multiply. God said that he created us on his image and that he also created Jesus in his image too.

If we are equal in identity to God, and Jesus is also equal to God by image, then we are equal to Jesus by both the inner and outer image.

Also, if Jesus was created with the purpose to heal, the purpose to command thing to happen, and they happened as he commanded them to be, then that is exactly what a man has to practice to perfect, practice to command.

Within him he knew and felt that his God. God image was his outer look.

- He walked like God; we have to walk the same as God too.
- He reasoned like God, what comes out of our mouth has the power to either heal or set a curse on others.

The son of God on his practice to perfection, behaved like God himself. Purposely it was God's aim for us to behave like him. Jesus comes to earth with one aim, nothing less or nothing more, but to practice perfection at its best.

God is very jealous to what belongs to him; he doesn't hesitate to punish even children for the actions that were carried out by their parents. Just like Jesus was beating those who where trading at the temple without hesitating, he did that to protect the image and the principles that the temple stand for. The principles specifically, imply that there is nothing wrong about one being jealous of what he has accomplished.

You've got to protect your territories. Should it happen that one enters without an authorized manners; such person has to be dealt with accordingly.

We give this guide line to make sure that people stop repeating the same mistake over and over. Our main purpose in this earth is to represent the image and the principles of God.

We need to forgive at all times and provide help when necessary, but we need to let people experience the real consequences of their action to the fullest. It is God's plan through struggling one for the victory of strengthened, so that those who pass the test of time can be able to realize the purpose of life.

In most case there is nothing wrong about punishing those who wrongs against us. Forgiveness has nothing to do with people just smoothly escaping the taste of what is their own medicine. The idea is to conform on God will, to practice perfection at its ultimate best; with the principle of letting others to purposely solve life mystery puzzle.

2. RE-BOUNCING

"Keep your mind, your eyes and your soul onto the big picture and on the other hand taking care of the consequences and benefits simultaneously".

Chele Mthembu

After any greater force applied, there must be an art brought about by mechanism of elasticity if ever an individual want to regain the shape before force was applied.

It is measure on the capability of going back to the original length after being stretched; it has every thing to do with regaining the well being after being squeezed.

Re-bouncing is self-confident manner of standing up, after having lost the direction in life. It is a principle category that one depends on it for his entire life span. Losing this principle is equals to the death end to one's life, death end to one's purpose. Re-bouncing is the principle category that governs both the inner image (brain and heart), and the other image like the physical appearance and strength.

When ever the tennis ball is in the court, both the player has to give their best. Beating the ball out of his side with the skills and greatest shorts, it is what he has to do best.

Due to receiving such shorts, when time goes-by the tennis ball loses its outer hairy cover, but its inner re-bouncing strength is retained. As long as the air is inside it, it maintains the strength to re-bounce despite the outer looks. Despite the beating and lose of its hairy cover, what keeps it going is what is within it.

Life is full of number of temptations. Due to what is called curiosity, we took some chances to touch and feel the heat of the burning coal and we got our fingers burned. It is the outer physical image that got burned, but the strength is within you for as long as the breathing is taking place you've got to bounce with the same capability done by the tines ball. It is the strong emotion, strong faith, and the inner-you that governs your existence, better that what your outer looks do.

Even when the outer hairy cover is removed, it does not loose its purpose of regaining the bouncing state of its art. Maybe you have made a bet on certain things and you lose on that bet. Get your self together brother; get your act together sister. We are not interested on how much and how you ended up losing on your game. You are the one who got your self in that situation, get your self out. Get out today. Just waste one minute longer and expect to deal with the consequences of having wasting that moment.

Failure to put self defense into practice immediately when the challenge arises, it is the first crack leading to the break down of the most detailed structure holding up the chemical solution need to up-roots the problem permanently.

Always kill the problem right from the main source before it spread like cancer taking over the body.

Take a great deal of re-bouncing effectively with the attitude of action now rather than later.

Some one is giving you the hart time, but you are scared to get out of that house, scared from being dependant to the state of independent. Be worn, to be scared kills your spirit, kills your attitude, removes all the efforts needed for creation of better future. At the end of being scared, your inner image is completely affected if ever not half death. You need your spirit to rank on the top performing level at all times, even when facing life threatening situation. The higher your spirit, the more you remain calm and at the right state of mind, that will enable you to make the best decision turning to guarantee better survival.

For the spirit to be at the highest level one need to have the courage to take bold steps even though time seems to be against him, even when the situation seem to be hopeless. No one knows what tomorrow hold for us, so why wait for the time that does not yet exist. Keep your mind, your eyes and your soul onto the big picture and on the other hand taking care of the consequences and benefits simultaneously.

3. IMPLEMENTATION METHODS

Your life is to be lived with the attitude possessed by the scientist and engineers, for every discovery they have made, is always a question of what next?

Chele Mthembu

God commanded, we took the command and did what we had to do, we multiplied.

God commanded, go out there and live by what you have sweated for.

Without any doubt in the mind we did what was commanded to us. When coming to implementation, a black man or a black woman, takes the number one position, they are the king of implementation, when coming to do what they are told to do. His own understanding comes with the reflection of the success of what he has implemented. Succeeding on what his been told to do, what has been interpreted to him, carries more wait than what need to be mostly interpreted be him, questioned by him and implemented by his own terms and purposely act the act of the mighty God.

Walking on tight rope of God's will, the model of implementation is to be done through questioning and developing interest on self concept, which is what we stand for. It is not good for the man to keep on living and up-holding the interest of others before his own. Developing interest in finding who you are, keep you motivated, the fact that you are motivated gives you batter understanding of playing your role in life more effectively.

The development of interest on knowing yourself therefore has to be through taking lessons about what works for your life. Your mentor in life has to be no body else but yourself. The reason being, the only person that you have to be like him is an individual, and that individual does not have any duplicate. This is the field that has nothing to do with the field of getting your-self a mentor in the field of business or the field of sports. A person has been given the capacity of becoming the engineer of his own life rather than his life engineered as the end product of others. Facts of not engineering our life as pacified by the almighty, make us the fake of what we where born to represent on earth. Your life is to be lived with the attitude possessed by the scientist and engineers, for every discovery they have made, is always a question of what next? It is the question like' what next' that has let to greatness, better individualism within us and what we will be tomorrow.

4. NAIL

"I'm I going backwards or forwards,
is decided by the choice taken"

Chele Mthembu

A handy man; an artist, the man of art, this is the man who is able to take the wood and crafts it to make a living out of it. Different parts, of different shape, has to be joined together to make one unit or an item.

One of the materials that are needed to get those pieces of wood together is called a nail. A handy man always know where to put the nail, it may not be visible but the whole structure of the item to stay stable and firm depends on that nails between those woods. The stability of the house depends on the kind of nails (screws) used. Your passion is gone, your faith has been tested, and the inner you seems to be death, paralyzed and all that is left is just the feeling of hopeless. It seems as if you are walking on the darkest night where there is no single star visible, without any moon light.

You want to take that step but there is no bit of courage left with you.

So what are you going to do, here is the formula to be taken for the step forward in situations like that, forget about the romantic worth like passion as a drive, forget about faith, but act as if you are death and the is no pain or any thing to stop you from going forwards. It is that step that is determining whether you go forwards or you remain neutral.

I'm I going backwards or forwards, is decided by the choice taken, and that very choice is the main nail to hold what is to be achieved as the step has been take forwards.

Between the passion, faith, hope and courage, there is one thing to help as from standing up and face life, when the going seem to be getting tough. That is the willingness to go on as if we are dead and there is nothing to refocus us on our course to wards our destiny. This usually does allow us to get out of our comfort zone.

5. CULTURAL CONSTRAINS, RE-DIRECTED

"I turn to believe that, the made-up of the value of a thing, is transmitted from its opposite thing considered to be of an immoral"

Chele Mthembu

What if the next biggest satisfaction in life is entirely formulated on the culture that we do practice?

What if, culture is life at its true meaning? What if, life, and therefore culture is a certain product, and that product is not classified by the practice or certain community or tribe? Think about it, maybe culture is not the color of the skin or just about some one trying to hard to fit on the believe of other.

Then that will mean, culture is something we have never realized, never thought it could be what it is. Culture is therefore explored to be the brain functioning to the fullest. If then, the culture of the mind doesn't subscribe to its free thoughts, then the bondage will be able to keep its legacy of existence, and that can happen only if the make-up object designed for it, is not on any project to find the escape road.

What is repeated time and again as the gravity of truth, whereas its not, make the escape road to be of the less value to what is it worth.

I turn to believe that, the made-up of the value of a thing, is transmitted from its opposite thing considered to be of an immoral. This thing, of the value transmitter, is the main reason the escape road needs its constrains re-directed

Even in the group of certain culture, no two people can have the same culture, they may be in the same practice, but their mind are complete different, as they subscribe to different kind of constraints re-directions and the value transmitters. That is the culture of the brain; the culture of an individual, when functioning to the fullest capacity, has to repeatedly produce a re-directed forceful character through such repeated re-direction of previous known constrains. Professor Muhammad Yunus, from the annual Mandela lecture once before said, "Dead culture is good for the museum, not for human society. Human society moves on, evolves and creates its own culture."

Deduced from that is, the capacity of human society in terms of cultural needs; has to be re-directed daily and it has to be an individual destiny, a calling to be strived for. What are you striving for? Create counter culture, should you practice relying on the past road not created by you, may lead you to un-satisfaction out-come. Redirect your course of action, find your escape road from the bondage of uncivilized method of determining one's existence, and keep moving on. Immoral is considered to be dead and not to be practiced, but people who are the rulers of this world are the greatest immoral practicing group. They use the culture of doing things, culture of thinking to bondage us from not entering the world of their control. You can not enter the world of control in any part of life if you are not receiving the transmitted value, from the immoral made-up exploration. It is not up to me to determine what is moral and immoral, but that is to be determine by either you blindly follow based on the constraints created by a dead culture, or you take on the desire and new method you can freely-so come-up with through freethinking to create your alive counter-culture for the purpose of control in life, as a right given by God to human being.

6. IDENTITY

"So many things have been said so often to us, about us and for us but very seldom by us".

By Steve Biko, black viewpoint (1972)

True identity is within. Identification of yourself first by your own point of view, matters better than how others view you. The relevancy of a true character can therefore be accurate, if the action of the man at first is not to the satisfaction of other man, the satisfaction of the creator of character has to come first, and has to be expressed without hesitation in both the action and newly discovered weapon of power, which is nothing else but the power of spoken words. It is the very same words that where used as a weapon to enslave the mind, by the time the master of slavery were identifying and categorizing based on inferior and superior. Hence it will take the very same power of spoken words to free the mind. But on this period, the words won't be from the mouth of the master of mind slaver, but it is going to be from the act of self-realization for self classification not driven by the formal education, neither influenced by the religion oppression in seeking a point of reference regarding its two irrelevant stated arenas, the arena of hell and heaven.

A person who approves his character, but only letting it to prevail after the approval of others has taken place, such person has committed an offence against the force of nature governing his existence. Only of this offence can the very same force make hell break loose and the person facing the consequence of being a coward due to giving-up his self governing identity to those he seek to please.

Identity assassination hence, take place when one centralizing his character to how others view and think about him. Failure to make self realization is regarded therefore as giving away self governing mechanism that nature gave to you to preserve, your individualism picture of existence. Take control of the re-birth of you identity on your own terms.

7. POWER

"A man who takes too long to make a killing for success, and his efforts produces greater benefits, has the reputation of patience"

Chele Mthembu

Potential, is what a goal setter, visionary man, a man in a path to create the reputation that really differentiates him from others. Usually put potential into good use. Your freedom is greatly based on your thinking and the level in which you put your potential behind you to be your driving force. Progressing in life has to be powered by potential. The study in East Africa has shown that for an African Fish Eagle to make a successful strike, it has to be powered by potential day-in and day-out for every perch executed. African Fish Eagle spend about eight minutes a day for actual fishing, the rest of the day spend being perched. This is simply meaning that, it takes a great deal of patience and practice, but about all trial and errors.

This is confirmed by the study that has reviled that for every successful strike, there were fourteen unsuccessful one. Out of fifteen trial and errors executed and putted to the test, only one strike produces results.

Fifteen trial and errors; all in a total of eight minutes, at the end of the day a strike has to be accomplished.

Keep your eye o the ball, you are about to make a striking at the least moment you expected. Your reputation has to be interrupted by how visionary you are and how great is your drive. Your drive and vision is interpreted by you and others through the kind of actions taken by you proportionally to the time taken.

A man who takes too long to make a killing for success and his efforts produces greater benefits, has the reputation of patience. Making a killing at an instance, gives the other man a reputation of being a go getter. This go getter doesn't waste a minute when coming to taking advantage of the presence moment. He has the reputation of planting the right seeds at the right time, and he gets full-grown rewards sooner than what others have expected. But at the end of the day, both man ends-up with the same reputation. Goal setters and goal achievers status, is how they are recognized.

8. LEADERS OF CIRCUMSTANCE

"A person is not created to hold one status for eternity,
hence, do not under estimate yourself
or the changes coming your way;
there is a fortune in every circumstance"

Chele Mthembu

The go ahead of "project combination" of ether a partnerships or a working force is made up of the circumstance re-explained from the onset of the project. It is not the duty of the leader to keep track of the positivity during the process of the project lifespan, the duty is basically therefore completed before the task begun.

In partnership like where the money is consent, the rich people are the masters taking advantage of the talented one. The talented one if ever selling himself cheaper, he is therefore considered to be committing an injustice to the leadership of circumstance.

The right owner of the product produced and also the owner of the talented group of people did justice filling the gap that the creator of the product failed to faithful. The advantage of the creator of the product is transferred at the end, creator becoming the servant of the right purchaser, the owner whom is supposed to be the servant becoming richer than the team of people whom is the one supposed to be rich. The power ownership is mainly lost by the people as they choose to be scared to exercise the presence according to "the power of being selfish. Selfishness for prosperity is not connected to loyalty of the past which is not working for an individual, but, it is an advancement of the power owner to further the interest of his own center.

The relevancy of the argument is much practiced by the 'African voters' in politics. These African voters are directly responsible for the future stabilization of the continent, but their loyalty to the so called former movement of freedom fighter, makes them to transmit the power of their vote cheaper to the cheapest bidder. In so doing failing to re-define the direction of the power they are holding.

These voters are given hands-outs weeks before time for casting the vote, and similarly become forgotten the very few weeks after casting their power. In the process the state of their future rest on one category of people's hands and the corrupt minded of one party.

The talented product producers and the African voters can learn something valuable to the married couples. As differently as this two may be, the state of being single is the most expensive one when compared to the state of marriage commitment. But the power is to be shared onto the partnership. Once the marriage lead to divorce, whatever that has been accumulated has to be share.

A person is not created to hold one status for eternity, hence, do not under estimate yourself or the changes coming your way; there is a fortune in every circumstance. Wake-up Africans, partner yourself and create the circumstance enabling you in the work-place and political movement, to make the break through in changes of power both locally and internationally. Time for dictatorship should be got away with.

9. ENGAGE

"Limiting your desire in life; by living below average,
like the definition of sin preferred,
limits the participation of the mind to be truly engaged,
on the base of transforming us to fulfill the
calling God intended for us".

Chele Mthembu

The engagement of the mind in the game of life ride after the freedom of choice. The mind has been oppressed with the false teaching about what a real sin all about. It is therefore been done to interrupt the process and role that the mind has to play in the execution of the freedom of choice in which it is only through the engagement of the mind that such execution can be reached. Sin is defined in taking one's live, rape and stealing.

The mind that is well engaged, ride after the concept of transforming its self. The only way that the mind can be transformed is by adopting the re-bouncing attitude of the tennis ball, in witch the capacity is maintained by going back to the original state after been squeezed. This attitude will interrupt and reverse the slavery oppression of the mind.

The mind has to be engaged in the game of choosing:

- Who we fall in love with.
- How many partners we can afford to be involved with and maintain their need and through protecting them.
- Our view to wards life, expressed without the influential averaged by the definition of sin.
- To ride with the engagement of the mind in decision making with great self-esteem.
- Above all, to ride with the pride that assures us that we will come out victoriously to the

other side of the struggle with the desired accomplishment. This is also powered by the 'I can attitude'.

- Limiting your desire in life; by living below average, like the definition of sin preferred, limits the participation of the mind to be truly engaged on the base of transforming us to fulfill the calling God intended for us.

10. SERVING

"Don't compromise knowing the real truth and practicing it, with the happiness of being praised and accepted simply because you are half serving"

Chele Mthembu

In the process of serving in line with the calling on earth, serve according to your calling.

There are three categories that one can serve within their parameters, namely:

Financial servers, emotional and physical serving

Financial servers

If your want to share you finance through distributing it, either by giving for the social need without expecting anything, then do so.

Should it be through having multiple partners through some form of mutual relationship, and protecting them against diseases, then distribute your money, financing the needs of those partners. It is your calling to serve in the sector of finance. Neither will it be a sin to be rewarded with the emotional satisfaction for having serving there. Never deny your self the satisfaction rightfully given to you by God. Any way, those whom are reaping the financial rewards on the side of darkness are those who God himself, gave them the treasure of hidden secret place, financing them, can not therefore considered to be a sin committed by the financer.

Emotional and physical serving

Your presence has to make the healing process to those who are at your surrounding both emotionally and physically. But for the benefit of physical well being, tell the truth. True healing comes with the art of preparing others mentally to be realistic and face the facts about what ever the situation they may find them self into.

Don't compromise knowing the real truth and practicing it, with the happiness of being praised and accepted simply because you are half serving, due to allowing your-self to be misused by others. A knowledge serving person, stand the grounds in which he serve within. He practically serves himself first.

The end product of that are the true identity and a real character of what his calling on earth stands for.

Only then, after finding his identity, will he be able to serve others knowledgably. This is the principle of 'first thing first'. Once this principle is done, then the emotion has been served, and its healing will transmit to the physical healing.

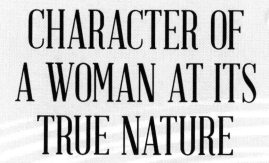

CHARACTER OF A WOMAN AT ITS TRUE NATURE

"Remember that in nature women can charge to any percentage, but that is mainly determined by how stupid is a man, and how he can lose his focus".

Chele Mthembu

It's for a while now, if not for along time for others, that relationships has been giving us a headache. We've got our heart broken; our spirit down, which then resulted on forgetting our part in the very same relationships. We went on and put all the blame onto others for the out come of the wrong relationship that we've got our self engaged in.

Our relationship in most case, are not really based on the concrete character at its main roots, as it is supposed to be based. It takes a great man or a woman with a great character, to tell what character is the other person within just few days. It is within the other person tone of the voice, the body language and the kind of different topics that one engages in, that gives us the whole picture about what are the content makes you.

You know once before, I was listing to a professional, in the baking sectors. He said to make the best tasting cake; you have to fallow the instructions carefully. It is the combination of all the ingredients that make the cake to be the best tasting one as desired. Nothing less or more is required.

- Should one of the ingredients be less, the cake will then be easily breakable.
- Should one of the ingredients be more, either way the cake will be breakable.

With that one concludes that, the best tasting cake with its smoothness requires nothing less and nothing more, for it to be better, as the baker preferred it to be.

A character at its best device movement of truth, movement of nature, is the same as this cake. A single person in most instances runs after the idea of finding a partner to be with, like a tail of the dog running after its head. The bad news for the tail in this scenario is that, the tail; will never catch up will the head in this racing. It is by this fact that, people who are single misses the required factors needed to build a strong and a steady relationship, that is as perfect as a bond between a mother and a child.

A relationship that a man and woman need to invest their life time onto it; if it is based on four individualism elements of character:

- Security—The first and by far most, the important factor that is based entirely on trust and honesty that the two keeps to avoid out-side forces interfering with their bond, without the knowledge of the other partner.
- Dignity—Your partner's appearance and attitude has to be the reflection of you. Although his is an individual at his own.
- Respect—Hiding numbers of other opposite sex people at work place so that your partner may not see them, it is not respect to your relationship

at all. For those who claim to be faithful to the marriage. For the single's, along as you haven't said I do, how you play is none of our business. Just don't bring disease home.

- Sense of belonging—A person has to feel and know that with you, by his side, you by her side, even if you are in the mist of no possibilities, you will find a break through to the other side of the tunnel.

Do not make an investment in a relationship if more than two of the above factors is lacking on you partner character. Wake up and stop chasing the wind. You rather be single and at your own than to be the walking corp. A hole where the mouse (rat) lives is always open. No matter how far or close the mouse distanced to the hole, when the going gets tough whereby the cat makes an attack, the hole will still be open to provide the security.

Same applies to our characters, if the going get tough in a relationship, the must be a way out.

Life has no guarantees, so always be prepared for the unexpected. It doesn't matter how good the relationship is at the present moment, never close the door to the state of being single again.

Enjoy the relationship, enjoy the present moment, after roll it is a present as it is, but, let the door to through to the state singleness always be like the hole of the rat, open at all times.

Let us explore what a woman stand for, the five differentiator's character, which is possessed by both the single and married woman. They are:

Winners
Organizers
Motivators
Achievers
Negatives

If you are a female person, this powerful character is within you. But only those who are practicing such five differentiators are getting at the forefront of their games. All women, as a kind of a clan, have been so much fortunate to have their character measured as being winner. A winner possesses the attitude of being highly motivated. Winners can see and feel the price, already on their hands, before they can even get on the journey to dig it out, even if it can be under the ground. If they have made up their mind to find it, it has to be found despite what they have to go up against.

When the situation seems to be conducive and positive enough, for her, she always has the triggering mode to turn out victoriously. In physical science it has been proven that unlike poles of the magnet do attract each other.

Whenever the situation seem to be positive, a woman natural will turn to be charging negative, that is the kind of triggering mode she needs in order to take advantage of the situation, in order to take the upper-hand in the game, visible to be played at a give sport by that time. A woman always wins the game before they can even take on the play mode. They win the game first in their minds.

The past teaching thought us that, in order to get ahead in life one needs to stay positive in all times. But as creative as she is,

A woman born a winner;

A woman born a motivated;

A woman born an achiever;

She will wait for the situation to charge positive like a hawk watching it's pray. Her triggering mode is as good and best as the technological timed triggering mode.

Top quality of a character of woman is mainly sustained by "O" which stands for organizing.

An organization comprises of a team of experts and strategic thinkers. But a woman as an individual, she is as equal in status as the organization formed with, a team of top minds.

- It takes a man with the real guts to have a relationship with a woman of the above character.
- Take a chance, and challenge a woman with the above character, a woman charging negative

without having to compromise her standard, and live you life in misery which can reach the state of depression.

Briefly let us explore the character of the man who qualifies to have a steady relationship or be in a challenge with a woman in possession and practicing her character at its true nature. The character of man is made up of "maturity, accuracy and negotiation" skills. These are the kind of skills making up the ingredients need, within the brain and heart to complete the man as the product God created. Only the person with the maturity, accuracy and negotiation above average qualifies as a skilled man, either you are having a beard full on your chin or not, won't have any effects on being the skilled one.

Marriage doesn't either reflect you as the one who made the better hunting; it may even expose you as the hunted one, categorizing you as the non-skilled.

Simply meaning, having beard or being married, you may still be just an ordinary school boy trying to find the balance in life.

Remember that life is just a game to be lived as one prefers. But the out come results are determined by the mental power made of a strong character.

There is no more room for trial and error in relationships and marriages.

We've got to learn to make thing happen. Relationship has to work and marriages have to last for a life time. So how can we make that to happen? Well that can be made possible by the man, as the hunted one.

Woman like things to go their way in general practice. But like I said, they are negatively charged, so to keep them in control, be matured by giving her the necessity requirements to charge herself. The only time that she will make your relationship miserable, is when you lose your touch of maturity that may lead her to below the level of charging mode.

Also, make a room for her to provide for you in any way she can. That will give her a sense of being valuable. Rather than objecting her, make her an equal partner, nothing more, nothing less than that. It is by that respect will she consider you matured.

Unfortunately, the state of accuracy in a relationship can not be kept into control by one partner, of whatever gender. Accuracy is attainable in this equation relationship; by none stop efforts of the two, whom are involved for mutual relationship. The so called 'equation relationship', can produce best results if one partner is lacking certain skill in life, and the other partner is helping while the one helped is meeting the helper half away willingly. The accuracy is more effective if, a woman is flexible on the element of motivation. Her motives in the skill of accuracy, have the energizing effects to keep the whole thing of togetherness fresh and above all, fun and undying.

During the time regarded as the phase of negotiation methods, whereby a man ask for mutual relationship from a woman, pay very careful attention when she say, she needs to think about your offer. Keep in mind that man turns to think that they are the hunting one for the woman, but in reality man hunt no one but themselves. Don't give too much of what you can offer, rather let her put her cards on the table first, and you work through them carefully.

If you put your cards first as a man, playing superman at the go, you are giving her enough rope to hang you, she will over charge negatively, and pull too much of what you can stand for. Remember that in nature women can charge to any percentage, but that is mainly determined by how stupid is a man, and how he can lose a focus.

Hence it is better for man to marry taking into consideration all of the four individualism elements of character discussed above. A person in lack of one or two of such elements can marry same person lacking according to his level. Do not marry a woman above your level of skill. At all times, she leaves her hole open with the capacity not to be filled for her entire life-time. She will negotiate her way out better than you do, and that will degrade you as a man.

ATTITUDE TO PENETRATE BOUNDARIES TO SUCCESS

"It takes the intelligent person to learn, but a fool is more comfortable with his stupidity and the idea of being the most ignorant person"

Chele Mthembu

Attitude is the spiritual form of living. A person who has mastered the art of it, his is always at the upper hand when coming to any kind of life chasing games. Every scenario he find himself, to him it appears to be just another game play. Taking advantage of what is in need of his attention, it's a pleasure to be explored.

Attitude is the way of thinking in relation to the given point. Attitude is the way of behaving in relation to the given point. I'm determined to be successful; I will be faced with the greatest red lines, boundaries to cross over, mountains to go up against, and no matter what kind of traps life may impose in my ways, with the silence attitude that I'm in possession of, taking advantage in relation to the given point is what I will do best.

Talking about that, the abdomen of the pregnant woman is bigger than the abdomen of the regular size of the women whom is not pregnant. A pregnant woman has life in her abdomen; it takes nine month for her to give birth. In the process of that nine month the body is getting busy to prepare the breast to get ready to produce milk, so that the minute the baby is born can be breastfed. Even if the size of the woman opening in which the baby has to use as the passage to the out side, seems to be smaller, the baby has to be out of the body coming end of nine month.

The other path might be provide, the baby must be out. Let as link this to an operating in destruction organization by the name of 'Terrorist Inc' under the leadership of Bin-Laden. The Terrorist Inc, had their mission silenced, underground planned for destruction. The abdomen of the Terrorist Inc was full of the kind of thinking, the kind of behavior, the attitude to make their operation well known by the entire world. To do this they went up against the number one, most capable in terms of security and technological status, the Unite State of America.

Mission dated: 11 September 2002

Mission named: Terrorist Inc Capability Testing

Success requires one to have the mind that operates like the abdomen.

These should be the mind that has the capability to be putted on the test of going the extra miles. This is the mind that is lining up with the behavior generated from the chain of events. Each of the events dated in every step of the way before they can even take place, success needs to be determined from smaller particles as they are produced and be added up to make the big picture.

Pregnancy as a process of giving life is dated. A Terrorist Inc, mission was dated. Our days in this world are numbered and dated by nature itself before death. But like the Terrorist Inc, it is up to the individual to have his chain of events well date. The day that the baby is born, the baby can feed from the body. The world is producing for a human being. But a man kind goes to bed with an empty stomach, majority remains poor, but the one thought to have created those suffering, had the nature well in plays to produce for his loved one. Amongst the hungry one and the poorest, you find the class of criminals. The world is formed mainly of three people, they are as follows,

- Advantageous, the benefiting type from nature production;
- Advantageous, closed out for left-over;
- Advantageous, making a way on the path rejected by the world.

From these three categories, advantageous benefiting type from nature production, and the advantageous closed out of the picture for left-overs, are the two type of class that the world has no problem of their existence. But the third category, advantageous, making a way on the path rejected by the world, has no room available for it existence. This last, third path, is in relation to the given point, for forcing a way out against all odds. It is the path made visible, felt and above all made alive by criminals. Just like pregnancy and Terrorist Inc does, criminal, they date and they name their mission.

Project date: Today

Project named: "Penetrating Boundaries To Success"

Remember that nature has our days in the world numbered, as much as anything can happen at any time, criminal are working on the present situation they are having most of their missions dated today. Penetrating form one point to the other requires great self comfort through the course of the process.

The morality of criminals has been put on the side of sinfulness. But of the due course they are able to have series of benefiting effects.

Criminal's way of thinking, way of behaving, in relation to the given sport, put food on the table of the police officer, and facilitate the finance school mattes of the security officer's child throughout years of academic. The soldier survival in terms of material benefit is due to the thinking and behavior of criminals. It is a stupid thing for a police officer to complain about the high rate of crime, actually it sound much the same as the officer saying, get those food out of my children's mouth so that my loved one can suffer. The person practicing as the private attorney will never complain about the high rate of criminal activities. In fact, lawyers are professional criminals.

Criminal activities are therefore benefiting the first type of category, advantageous, the benefiting type from nature production. Criminal mind is the natural thing, it is a talent. Engineers make the technological equipments, and criminals are available to re-engineer such devices.

In the process providing the mechanism of getting them improved, for that, one is getting the value for what his paying for when the price of the device is increased.

It is up to the individual how they choose their thinking to wards criminals. I was just stating my point of view base on my take on freethinking. On top of that, this is the task in which all the concepts needing redefinitions are worked through.

What is it that one can do, to get things done beyond the extra ordinary performance, even through it is not the principle accepted by the world society at large? It is simply by getting my soul impregnated as the base of abdomen, and for that, giving life to other, especially to the advantageous, closed out for left-over class. On the long run; one way or the other, reaping the benefit of your efforts has to take place. How will the benefit be like, it is up to life to determine.

This analyzes how tough competition is out there. The competition in life taking into consideration the three types of advantageous discussed above, it is the deference between two sides. The side of starving and then throwing in the application latter for the death certificate although you are right in the middle of food, or the side of taking and eating for the purpose of surviving for as long as you possibly can, not forgetting number of days given by life calendar to you.

When you find yourself in the middle of this line, line of taking one side, just let your mind trigger which side to take, then follow the lead of the line to where you find a turning point or another two different path leading to two different direction. If ever you have chosen the difficult path once, then, when you arrive onto this two departure ways taking separation from the main path that led you there, then do not choose the easy one simply because it shows that majority have traveled over it time and again. Let you choice ride on its first original uniqueness.

In its mission an insect trapping flower, it has its jaws operating like a team. Insects are the smallest pray, for that matter, it takes the best organized team to trap one. Once it is triggered, this flower jaws closes in a special way like two hand fingers putted together between one another. As small as the insect, once one jaw is not functioning well, there is a greater chance of the insect getting escaped.

It is the same as the family member who lost the attitude towards the functioning of the family as one team. The slightest problem can have what it takes just like the missile to un-earth the roots of the whole unity. The abuse of substance like alcohol has the same weight of destruction. It can have the marriage or the relationship putted to pieces and beyond reconciling.

For the power of the unit to be on terms of good performance at all time, be there, be a real player. Do your part on what has to be taken care-off by you. Be the team player in relation to the given point at all times. Whatever a trap has to be carried out, do not disappoint other committed members. If you do, then you are the weakest link to be taken care of before the team can even think of getting rid of the problem.

In a workplace, the person who is not punctual, cripple the spirit of the whole team. Whenever the big task is broken into smaller tasks and a particular portion is been assigned to you, failure to deliver on or before the death line, also have the same crippling of the team spirit. Either you are late with an hour or ten minute on the delivery, put the stigma of unable and incapable team.

The best player prepare before hand for the brainstorming sessions.

The best player has the capacity to expand the smallest idea, to become the year number one winning capital generating idea in the company profile.

It takes the intelligent person to learn, but a fool is more comfortable with his stupidity and the idea of being the most ignorant person.

An intelligent worker knows how to separate the work time from the family time.

And also, intelligent worker knows that it is best for one to be on the list of best performers, listed on the boss record books. The good records you kept determine the relationship between you and your boss.

The one, who is ignorant, does not understand the important of having a name on the winning team. The benefits that comes with it, is the joy in the work environment improve gradually. The team spirit over-come the hard angle when the team comes across one.

In simple terms, intelligent workers are driven by motivation, powered by the knowledge of using the given sport accordingly for their benefit.

Back again to the Terrorist Inc, the Alcaida, led by the world number one masterminding man, Bin-Laden, had a special way of doing things. In the attack carried out on the eleven September. They have had the brainstorming session that was named 'project unusual technique'. As much as one will not want to think of what have happened during that time, we must take a path to travel inside this Terrorist Inc mind. This is to determine what was going on their thinking by that moment; we must find out, was it to prove a point leading to be taken serious by the world, or was it anger? I guess it was both of the factors, which is proving a point and anger.

Project unusual technique had two sports.

One, anger in relation to a given sport

The Terrorist Inc, due to anger, they have converted the passenger jet to the most capable fighting jet for destruction. Due to anger, they knew that lives where about to be lost but they putted their own first on the line. Two, proving capability in relation to a given sport, they, launched an attack to a country with its own equipment, an iron machine flying against the wind like and eagle. They took the equipment that was already accessible for the mission.

The second analyzing of project unusual technique, matches with the path followed by the sex worker. Instate of going corner to corner searching for material to earn a living, they took what is read and abundantly available for generating cash. That cash generating mechanism is basically their artist bodies. In doing so, stating the point that the road to penetrate the boundaries to success has no limit at all.

Also on this matter, western countries are not better than Terrorist Inc; these first class countries give donations to Africa, after corruptly taken from this continent. They put their power in place to invade other countries illegally, in matters of morality determined by the society.

Terrorist Inc and the rich western countries are not deferent. They are both inflicting pain on the lives of ordinary people. In principles, the two are the same as the avoided arena of hell, and the fantasized arena of heaven, they can not be considered operating free from each other. Rich western country leaders (particularly the United State of America and Britain, the former colonial master of my African country) did no justice for the world as much as the likes of Bin-Laden together with Saddam Hussein also didn't. They are all the devils most powerful clowns with the capacity to really make their presence to be felt, against any legal boundaries existing and having made to be obeyed by the so called developing countries only.

The first analyzing of project unusual technique is behind over trusting, one can have onto others. Those who are anger to you, at the later stage will convert the trust you had on them to be the fighting machines to get rid of you. Any way, in this world there are price to be paid, either in a painful or happy feeling. Don't trust with a blind eye.

In the book, 'The Biography Of Bin-Laden' it has been stated that, Bin-Laden never had a complete trust on his troops concerning his hidings. For that reason he did not stay in one place for a long time. He had the strategy for staying in different hiding places. But on the other hand, the opposite man on the book 'Julius Ceesser' the man himself, had too much trust to his conspirators, the very same people got rid off his life for good. Both of the techniques used by these two men are different in a sense that Bin-Laden survived.

The Africans citizen through the entire continent, they are to be blamed for such a mineral producing part of the world, to be one of the poorest. Failure to refuse tyranny practice by the majority of leaders in this part of the world is the main weakest link amongst the Africans. Leaders are in a continuous basis, makes pathetic deals with the foreign countries, baring in mind the interest of such countries before the interest of Africa as a whole. Instate of Africa to make a point, it take the back seat of becoming the state of left-over. This has been done so by trusting, believing and fearing that its existence is dependable to the foreign relations, on terms stipulated by such foreigner as a capitalist.

The executive committee of the Terrorist Inc was made up of top minded people. The technique used by the Terrorist Inc executive committee for taking action was risk associated. The results you've got, up to so far, was related to the kind and measurement we have taken based on the risk associated with our actions. Best results are reserved for people with the heavier capability, enabling them to go against the waves of the air like and eagle, and be able to resist the pulling force of the gravity while rising to the top.

As it has been done on "project unusual technique sport one; anger in relation to a given sport", the Terrorist Inc, due to anger, they have converted the passenger jet to the most capable fighting jet for destruction. How about we Africans, just like the 'Terrorist Inc' we became under the influence of hunger and differently convert the picture of our existence in the world, to make us known for what we are really meant to be in relation to a given sport.

The given sport authorized by the state of poorness, in relation to its capacity awaiting destruction of selfness benefiting a foreigner, to be replaced by the nature of life, underneath the status of selfishness. This will be intended to make Africa pregnant, so that, after destruction of the state of poorness, Africa can give birth of wealth capable of sustaining one generation to the other, and free from consuming donations shaming a character of a man to receive.

If ever you have not made it as you have planned in the past. Maybe it is time to take some few steps; it can be two or three steps back wards.

Examine your life executive committee, it comprises of your lover, your children and your best-friends. These are the team of people who should be keeping you motivated at all times, when the going is right on the track and when the going is getting tough. In fact these people are the different paths when united in your life, making the one united paths enabling you to penetrate smoothly through the red line of boundaries separating poor environment with the rich environment for life fulfillment.

Life executive committee is made up of the most four mental do-able process. The only person at the forefront to make this process work is you.

It takes one person to guard

- The untenable abdomen, to produce life, that's the mother. Take care of this person; she's the pillow of your life;
- The untenable trigger, to trigger the abdomen to deliver live, the work of natural hormones. Whatever nature gave you, preserve it for eternity. Failure to do so lead to suffering as Africa has failed and is suffering to pay the price of its failure at present.
- The untenable and standing by team, to receive life delivered by the abdomen after the triggering mode has occurred. Here requires all family members' efforts. If the leaders, both in family and government, are failing to deliver they need to be removed for better option of leadership.
- At last, the intelligently well positioned plan to sustain life break through. This method is achieved through the knowledge of taking into consideration that selfless comes after selfishness, meaning the foreigner as a capitalist, his interest comes after our own in terms of exports in relation to what belongs to an African.

For the mind to function best, let its engineering purpose prevail over when given the risk associated task to take care of. Do not just believe what you are told; first take a test drive to see if what you are offered is in line with your engineered enable environment. Be very choosy of what you are attracting in your life, don't gamble up until you know the rules of that game. Know how such under-taken game can profit you either knowledgeable and materially, keeping in mind that a human being is not like any animal, knowledge and value of commodity is what keeps us going.

FAMILY AS A FUNCTIONING UNIT

". . . . No matter how much welcoming can you be
in the unit, guards against older secrets that the family
has been upholding and protected for many years."

Chele Mthembu

Nature has allowed a woman to bring life in the world, and that all her off springs initially cooked and natured in one womb. In other words, these off-springs were initially born as a unit. A unit in a sense that they shared the same blood, they have also shared the same warmth, from the same womb.

All of them had the chance to breast feed one at a time from their mother. One person who had carried them for a period of nine month, each one of them had the chance to experience with others interruption, his nine month period.

This chance was given to the last born child by the older ones before him.

They gave the last born the chance to share the blood of their mother at his own pace, to breast-feed at his own pace, but above all to experience and feel the warmth that belonged to them previously.

Brother and sisters were all born as a unit. The best unit operates as one, no matter the external interference. Once again, the best team of soldiers in a mission operates like a unit. In their penetration to the most dangerous building, each and every member of the unit has nothing to worry about his back. In this unit, you are most certain that your back is well cover and beyond any doubt, highly protected. You were not born with this people, you did not have the same warmth from the same mother, same womb, you share no blood, and you neither had the same breast feeding from the same mother. But you can bet your life in the protection of this unit in any dangerous situations, in which you can easily get killed at any time.

You can trust this unit better that you brothers and sisters, people whom nature had prepared them for your own protection when you need it the most, and at all times to cover your back.

Where did the chain get broke, what went wrong? We are about to do our own analyses based on the morality taught to us, from birth to adulthood. A brother has to remain a brother, no matter what he may come up against. A sister has to remain a sister, no matter the difficulties imposed to her by this man made life dominating rules.

The characteristics of the family as a unit, are entirely based on the unchallenged bond formed by nature, over extensive period of years. A person is not supposed to go to bed with the empty stomach, while his brother has enough bread to give him a slice or two. A sister can not be experiencing any kind of abuse from her boy-friend or husband while his brother is still alive and kicking.

A bread winner of any unit has to see to it that day-in and day-out, from the morning dawn to the evening, there must be some thing on the table to feed on. A brother in the family has the same status as his father to wards the family. A well groomed and matured brother, is the one who has what it takes to take over the entire family as a unit, after the father past away from this life.

Even if it happens for a mother to get a step father for them, it is the duty of the son to make sure that the dignity of his father's legacy is protected and lives on. Should your mother or any young one's to you living on poverty whereas, you are alive and intentionally ignoring your responsibility, then help God you don't deserve to be holding the title "brother", in this life. You where better off born without any other brothers or sisters, simply because you don't deserve them.

Respect is not something you demand, it is one of the most valuable thing that you have to earn through your words and action.

A family is better off without a brother who has turned his back onto other off-springs of his own unit. Before you go out there to try to impress other people, you need to go back to you roots, your home, your family and relatives to earn there respect first. It is better for a man to invest to other members of the family before he can invest to his partner, at any time that person may be out of your life.

A brother, who has a partner in most cases, has the unending bill to pay to the one he loves. The bill is all about buying time to stay much longer period with her. In return, thinking that his in control of his marriage, were as the truth of the matter is that, his not even closed on succeeding in relation to that mental ego. A woman truly respects a man who can go all the ways to protect his mother and sisters.

The community respects the man who has first gained the respect of his family as a unit.

Operation of the entire unit is based on every-one or aspect that forms part of that unit. For a brother to stay as a bread winner and head of his fathers off spring, for a brother to uphold the respect of the family, as a unit, a mother has to welcome the daughter in law with a warmth hands in the family as a unit. Sister also, has to make sure that, the very same sister-in-law feels at home, as a part of the complete functioning unit. But beware, no matter how much welcoming can you be in the unit, guards against older secrets that the family has been upholding and protected for many years. The secrets just like they where secrets before she came into the picture, they will remain to be the secrets.

Welcoming has nothing to do with opening-up, forgetting that, she may be a person not here to stay, but just passing by at any time. Disclosing too much to either the son-in-law or the daughter-in-law is the same as, giving that out the right ammunition powerful enough to completely make the family unstable at any time he chooses to do so.

Dare to disclosed them and bare the consequences of your action at the later stage if not sooner. The respect that has been uphold by the family as a unit, the better operation of the unit, have got compromised by us, in most cases due to having become too much welcoming.

- People, who have been holding the best recipes in different business, have generated great reward. They have earned respect. Their business has been operating for decade. The quality of their recipe can not be compromised, or get stolen due to the fact that they have kept the formula a secret.
- To uphold your character, keep your formula a secret. People says that talking about things do help, be careful, they may not all be interested on your well being, but on your secret.

Once the secret is in the open, the operation has been compromised, and it is the same as the wall of your house structure being fallen and you being as naked as the day you were born.

Trust, is all about throwing the results under stronger team. You don't just throw you results with a blind eye. You don't throw them on top where every one can see them with a naked eye. You have to throw them in a manner that you mostly put you last seed on the most fertilized soil, the soil that is rich enough to give you the best results, with increased seeds at the end of the harvesting season. The soil is as much important as the strong team that you trust enough to throw you results under it.

Trusting too much can be fatal. Even on the family as a unit some of the member can not be trusted with sensitive secret. It's better to trust you mom, but based on her character. Trust you father, depending on his principles to protect his family members.

Only the brothers with the real quality of brotherhood, a mother with good principles, same as the father, are the people that can be trust. Such brother, you can throw result under strong team, led by him without fear of getting you back stabbed for his own gain in the future, or make thing difficult for you when the going get tough in life.

Health, it is all about the secret of "healing aspect life throws harder" at you. When thing fall apart for a brother in a family as a unit, a sister has to be there for a brother every step of the way, when life had thrown harder difficulties to handle along as a human being. The health status of a brother has too much importance as much as the health of the sister has too much impotence to the brother.

A sister provides a sense of security to the brother emotional break dawn. If a brother has ill-health, it is the duty of the sister to see to it that the brother state of mind and emotional heal, by providing the soft sport healing a woman got from God.

The greatest emotional healing possessed by a woman as a gift is not only for her husband, but also for her brother. When it come to the emotional state of breakdown of the brother, a sister takes over the family as a unit, up until the state of the breakdown of the brothers emotion is back to normal. In the process of all of this, it does not matter what a sister has to do, she has to do what ever a woman has to do.

I'm not suggesting any immoral thing here, what I'm saying is that, people who had victory on what they have set their mind onto, did what ever they had to do for their success to be attained. They did not leave any thing to chance. They have pushed for opportunities, not to wait for life to present them, they made digging for survival. Even when the time was not on their side, when they felt down, they couldn't stop doing what they had to do for the unit to function at it best level. A sister and a brother working to gather for the well being of their family's, they don't believe in 'we almost did it', their main aim is to do it, once it is done, it has to go on non-stop.

This way, it will make a difference on 'healing every aspect life thrown harder" on both of them, ether emotionally or physically. If you are brother and sister and not taking care of each others emotionally or physically protecting each others needs, then you are, or might by the reason the family as a unit is not functioning well.

It is time to do something. The best time is right now, go sit down and have a detailed strategic thinking, which will enable you to have the attitude to penetrate the boundaries to success. Efforts are what it takes to have a brother accomplishing his mission with a high note. For him to stay focused and well on top of the game, a sister has to be the energy required to drive up mountains for the efforts his brother put on his own wife, kids and the other off-springs of his father. The input energy the sister puts in; has the influences; and determines the out-put results. Both brothers and sisters must have the rules of the game changed around here.

Results orientated, must be the name of the game. Commonly they share the same blood, they have also had the same breast that they previously expected it to produce milk for them, and the breads just did that for both of them, a brother should therefore have a will power to provide efforts which is both emotional and physical, and a sister should therefore have a will power to provide the emotional support for his brother. And both taking into consideration their health and trust in operational unit. Both with the same mind that is results orientated, either a relationship or a marriage falls apart with their partners, they are having each other to protect the unit.

At the end of the day, it does not matter what happens out side the unit, they both get the satisfaction of being results orientated based on a family as a unit. They both have what it takes to turn the impossibilities into possibilities. Genesis 19 verse 32, "come, let us make our father drink wine, and we will lie with him, that we may preserve seed of our father" those where "Lot two daughters" associating with risk taking. After roll it was God's plan for a unit to functions as one. The consequences did not limit the legacy of this two daughters unit. How you live you life is entirely up to you, because God gave all; he broke the limits of life at the time of Adam and Eve era.

THE POWER
BEHIND SILENCE

"A leap of faith in most cases is taken by the people who are wild enough. Wild necessarily implies that 'Wisdom Including Leadership Development'."

Chele Mthembu

At every time when the dog is bucking. On its bucking there are always two statements to be taken into consideration and to be analyzed.

The first statement, does it have the guts to make a bit, does it exercise its right of the strength to the fullest to courageously take a bit that will be labeled as a sign of the dog that gabbed the power, the power that authorized it to be the best differently trusted home security.

Secondly, it's just a dog that bucks without the guts to make a bit. Is it just a dog that bucks for making the noise that is not even results driven, is it bucking without being results orientate.

What do we have in common with a dog?

There are tow types of strategies that a dog with the guts to bit uses, or it may choose one of such strategy of the two.

Do we have the capacity to make choices in our lives? The first strategy the dog will make itself noticeable to give the attacked individual the chance to prepare himself.

This is the kind of a dog that likes the challenges from its opponent. The problem that may arise here is that, this dog can go back from its mission with its tail wrapped between its legs.

Same in life, if a person in life give the problem the chance to grow bit by bit, his risking experiencing the disaster that could have been avoided. You have noticed a problem, all you have to do is to take action to have it kill directly from the roots.

Why are you making a noise about it? What are you expecting to gain from that noise after roll? Noising about is risking to become a fool, it is considered therefore, as the basic step of applying to have your weakness noticed unstructured by others.

There is nothing wrong about going to the right people and ask for help, but making excuses about time and again is not an option. We don't want to hear about it any more. Tell us what went wrong; tell us what's strategies you are currently applying, how far are you, what is it that we can do in particular, related to what has already been done.

Take for instance the partner that is having an affair. What is the massage behind his or her action, it simply implies that such partner can

"Afford Future, Failing and Impossible Relationship" such person is having with you. Hence the person decided to ride on the movement of passion without having to wait for the impossibility at the future. The movement of passion, allow the present to deal with the future hazard.

Arguing about it and fighting is basically a risk taken, to expose your weakness on the open. Once the person knows your weakness makes the means to take advantage of them. So why bother arguing like a dog burking without the guts to take a bit. An affair simply translates the means that the other partner who committed it, he saw the future already failed with you. The relationship between both of you had the impossibilities of continuing at the present moment he executed the affair.

A point has already been made, so stop making a fool at your-self, by fighting and arguing about something that has already gone, already loosed. Never give the person the satisfaction of taking advantage of you before you have the guts to put an end to the hurt you are experiencing.

Later you will learn about the strategies that are needed to deal better with affairs.

The second strategy, a dog makes is attacking silence. In this kind of strategy, an opponent is not given the chance to prepare; the strategy here is that the problem is not given the chance for it to respond. An attack is launched here in a manner that is mostly referred to as the under ground attack. It is entirely based on the silence operation. When these kind of attack is launched, the dog pays a careful consideration to it's foots steps. Each and every step taken has to be silence to the ears of its opponent. Attach here is not made face to face. This kind of a dog has learned the art of grabbing the authority to execute the power first before its opponent. This dog has learned from its master that the"

The power behind silence deals better with any situation".

- The one taking advantage of you does that with the knowledge that his doing something under the ground, meaning that what ever his taking advantage off in you, is something his well gating away with. The time you realized what his been doing, your will be the one that will have to deal with all the consequences of his actions.
- His mind secretly operated silence, when he capitalized on your weakness.
- His actions are carried out silence, while his making fool of you and at the end, his is the one who will get all the satisfaction.

The "strength implemented logically immediately elaborate." Why the strength need to be logically implemented? Simply because, strength grab the power it produce when immediately implemented. When the plan is silence implement, immediately and logically, while the mind is in its peak level, takes you near courage to elaborate. The courage, to effectively make the best of every situation you find your self in. The strength is basically one of the best," System thoughtfully reacting effectively and naturally trusted health". A dog which attacks silence, immediately implement logically the" System thoughtfully reacting effectively and naturally trusted health". The strength and courage that this dog has is based on the natural mind, not its physical strength.

The battle field is completely in the mind. The out come of every action you take, both in a personal life or a corporate world, is determined by the state of your mind. When the mind takes control in a persons emotions, and a person's heart. Then the mind always takes the upper hand of getting the best at a give point of challenge.

Your emotions can sell you cheaper to others if your mind is not taking control. Your attitude happens to be your best weapon when you mind is in control.

Courage is deeply embedded on your state of mind. When the mind is in control in most cases you end up having all the necessity to take a leap of faith.

A leap of faith in most cases is taken by the people who are wild enough.

Wild necessarily implies that" Wisdom Including Leadership Development".

Taking a leap of faith is about developing a leadership and having wisdom as the product of such development. Wisdom is one of the best securities a person can ever have.

A wise person chooses his battles very carefully. He never underestimates his opponents just like a dog that attacks silence. A wise person knows that there is a power behind silences. He knows that silence deals better with any situation. Silence is the refusal to betray the secret. It is by these facts of refusing to betray the secret that make him chooses his words very careful when ever he speaks. His is very influential, both by his spoken words and body language. There is no body that can have what it takes to read him like a book, he keep his enemy and close friends guessing about what is his next move in life, based on his vision, goals and ideas, but one thing for sure, they all know him with on quality which is, his a man of his own kind. Are you wild enough to be a person of his own kind?

A person wild enough believe in developing a leadership inside extensively. A leader, who has developing a leadership inside extensively, doesn't lead by quarrelling to his fellow workers or staff member. It is the kind of person that he is, what his stand for, his body language, his dressing coat, and the kind of leap of faith executed by him, that command respect.

It is by this inside extensively that makes his position in his organization to come after his developed a leadership inside wider. His therefore not respect based on the position he hold at work or the kind of formal qualification his holding, but by the contents of his heart and mind set.

For better leadership in organization, friendship and family matters, a leader has to exercise maturity on thinking. In doing that, he will reap the reward of getting advantage of "improving opportunities near success" in every aspect of the field his leading. In general, exercising maturity on thinking, improves opportunities near success.

This is the kind of our today's leaders need to possess, we are tired of the kind of leadership that seem to be out dated due to tiredness that is obviously present it self from those who are at the fore frond. No more formal education to be the only factor that determine the person to be the near perfection king of a leader we need for all fields of life aspects.

We need a new tool, the kind of a tool that is well developed from an early age to the state of adulthood. The new tool is based completely on the fact of exercising maturity which improves opportunities near success.

This tool is baked up by the first and one of the greatest weapons one can develop at an early age, which is developed leadership inside wider. By exercising good ad health leadership, one improves his staff morals.

Improved moral among the staff increases productivity.

Developed line of communication has a great impact on productivities as well. Both the good moods in moral and the open line of communication in the work place, benefits the health of the entire staff in any organization.

Implementing maturity on thinking, rate you highly among your staff members. You may not give a damn about what your staff is thinking. But at the end of the day, that pay-check and your company success rely on the good health of your staff. It does not make you a great leader if people are suffering emotionally under your leadership style. Get a grip man, put people's health first, both your company and your success will be multiplied with folders better than the present moment.

THE REMAINS

Sustained by the one hour habit

"The one tool that one needs for greater achievements is to put into practice methods of, breaking-away from the present, whereas he is still at the present era itself."

Chele Mthembu

Having been taken from your place of origin, the value added in your life, the value that is priceless. The added value, which does not benefits in any-way in your life, but benefiting the live of others. Those were the treasure of Africa, those were the men and woman of Africa, taken to the other part of the world, these were the former slaves of different part of the western countries of the entire world. They had their attitude captured, which really got their heads down and their voices not heard. It is the history of the black man on his existence on western countries, the era of being both physically and mentally enslaved. He left what is known as the remains behind. History made him to exit the western countries through living the capable, natured remains with the idea that the day will come where by the very same left out remains will hatch the shell and lead and govern the former master of slavery, which is the super power state which is the United State of America.

The idea of playing the puzzle; history against the present, the present against the future kind of a game, has a direct link to the history embedding itself to the present. And how the present is attaching itself with the super glue to the future era, explains what is known as the remains finding its way to the movement of passion.

If ever you are the tertiary student at the present moment or you are the one on the junior position on your work place or any level you find yourself in. The one tool that one needs for greater achievements is to put into practice methods of breaking-away from the present, whereas he is still at the present era itself. This is the secret practiced before by the greatest innovators.

Here is how they did it, in every twenty four hour a day, they divided the day into potions.

The first potion; consisting of twenty three hours. It is the potion that accommodate.

- Seven hour of sleeping.
- Twelve hours of strategizing, striking deals and doing most of the events that has to do with ether the work, carries related matters and including personal stuff.
- Four hours is for complete relaxation, the time to maintain good health.

There is an hour out of the twenty four hourly making the complete circle of the clock wise. For life time, one simple hour the ordinary people will spent it for eternity not seeing its significant or priceless, the greatest leaders in the field of finance, or rather the creation of wealth, call it "The one hour habit"

The one hour habit, a specified hour a day, a sixty minutes of deep thought, it is signified by the weight is carries, the weight translating as "not good enough". Each day, sixty minute is used meditating about the present era. Although the current product or career may be of satisfaction to you, the twenty three hours may be used enjoying the benefit of having achieved such goal in your life. But sixty minutes, just one hour, deeply thinking through how improvements can be accommodated, influences the other direction that lead to personal growth, reaching the orientated state of the vision and emotional enriched satisfaction.

Personal growth state of reputation

The idea behind the though of any improvement for the brand change in the making has to bring in, the reputation onto some individual inheritance.

Orientated state of vision, for project new era, is on the top, as the personal growth state of reputation is the base for its structure. It is the means in which the modification of

'Detailed strategic thinking' is enhanced (see page chapter 3, ten points of the impossibility made possible)

The project new era, for orientated state of vision, for personal growth state of reputation, is a special principle that enables the desired out come to be acceptable. The results can be either, positive or negative, good or bad, it does not matter at all, simply because the bad and negative side provide the room for modification of rich environment to be found after the completion of 'project new era'. Project new era is the reality of life, it the thought that diverse the new set of circumstances that a man was created to live his life solving for.

The remains are the capacity found between each space provided by 'the fourteen imperatives to decolonizing the mind'. Let's go to the part next page as if we are opening the other chapter of our lives, chapter of imperatives.

FOURTEEN IMPERATIVES TO AUTHORITY

"The complexity of power existence in an individual can only be acquired, when an individual or a group is associating their existence with risk taking aiming at gaining authority"

Chele Mthembu

1. DESTINY CALLING FOR AN AFRICAN

The African writer for that matter said "Yes, the regeneration of Africa belongs to this new and powerful period! By this term regeneration I wish to be understood to mean the entrance into a new life, embracing the diverse phases of a higher, complex existence. The basic factor which assures their regeneration resides in the awakened race-consciousness.

This gives them a clear perception of their elemental needs and of their undeveloped powers. It therefore must lead them to the attainment of that higher and advanced standard of life".

By Pixley ka Seme

2. ERA OF NEW POWER

"The main practice that is said to be liberating us
is the very same practice, which is leading to
inferiority of a human being."

Chele Mthembu

The previous generation, the present generation and the future generation, can not afford to be riding on the same path, should they ride on the same path; that will mean the generation after the other have no means of its own era of power. The era of new power is the integrations of the old means of living together with the new one. African, it is time that we protect each other against the previous eras that have taken a lot from the black man. The remaining influence of such era should not be maintained in such away that, generation after the other is not affected in the direction of inferior practice. The main practice that is said to be liberating us is the very same practice, which is leading to inferiority of a human being.

The practice that is leading to inferior is therefore maintained due to the fact that we bow down to whatever it is said that is the path we should be traveling in terms of thinking and behaving. The terms of the superior, live and shine through us those who refuse to make a seize of "attainment of that higher and advanced standard of life" as (Pixley ka Seme) has said in that manner, the superior terms, if left unchallenged, rules the mind of those who unchallenged his terms, and advancement of his elementary needs, hence suppresses the developmental of an individual and community powers respectively. We are the awakened power in Africa; let us therefore realize that, as individual and communities at large, we are powerful enough not to bow down in such away that, the influence of the so called superior rules can shine through us. Africans, let us seize a clear perception of our elemental needs, we owe it to ourselves and the future generation.

3. COST LEADING TO TREASURE

"The right ending of any kind of the move is mainly embedded onto its initial ability to destabilize, the level of thoughts negating the effectiveness of mankind, as the custodian of his life".

Chele Mthembu

In the making of custodian power model of doing things, the cost of life negate with the attained value of thought, feeling and natural model of keeping thing the same. Negation is there in mankind, so that the very same mankind becomes the God's of mover and shakers creating the cost in life which its move result in changes and satisfaction in the custodian of life. Do not fear the holes and scares of mistakes created by you or others in your life; hold onto them as a capital, they are the cost you need to treasure in life. They are basically the leads to 'free power'.

As you gain ownership of different reference of wrong doings, you will also become the priceless specialist of free power, as it fit to the pieces of others people's puzzles, new life solution in created and attainable. Find where your previous mistakes can fit, once you do, cash it in any way to the highest bidder. Mistakes and their cost make's up the free power, enabling me to be God of new solution required by mankind. Do thing your way, there is a cost leading to treasure within your way, no matter your plans out-comes, there is someone out there who will be in need of your development.

4. ORIGINALITY AND ITS NON-EXISTENCE

"Catch-up with time, don't wait for it to catch-up
with you first, it is therefore better for you to do
things differently than the former mentally
oppressed generation, you are free"

Chele Mthembu

Theoretical yes, one can come up with the original work, but the non-existence part of it, is the most important side. We human being turn to kill the originality, if ever exist because I can not negate it, as it is already on the mind. But we kill originality by trying to keep it original.

The real power is in its non-existence. The identical made-up version of things makes their originality to exist, as the mind keeps the picture of existence. My point here is that, the value of originality comes from the non-existence. Hence without its opposite version, it won't be valuable. It is by this point that you need to loosen-up. Rather than valuing the original, value its non existence. Don't necessarily keep its picture in the mind, seek its non existence that leads to the movement of passion as on this era of events, new diverging of invention such as thoughts and material are devised embracing to the original and older thoughts and material. The main idea that people are having in their mind regarding the existence is portrayed on their physical being, but the real you is relaying onto your non-existence, your thoughts.

Strive to build the physical you on what others can not touch, by creating the system of the identical made-up version of things, making the system of individualism to be controlled only by you. In that way, you won't be subjected to killing your originality by trying to keep it original, due to attempting to please the society. Let the identical version of the expectation of those who surround you motivate you to find the non-existence of yourself. Doing that will produce the feelings of finding out the new mechanism or the methods that may make you a better lover, father, mother or leading to the improvement of the society you live within by becoming the role model of his own kind. Your non-existence feeling to find that other version, if you make it the endless efforts, it will in return also produce the endless results both in personal and professional relationships.

Those who are striving to keep the original versions of them-selves based on how they do things and through their thoughts and emotions, are to be careful of getting bored of life at an early age. Time will also catch-up with them in terms of being old to change in relations to doing things differently. The bad news is that, love matters will suffer at the end of becoming bored of daily routine which are unchangeable.

Catch-up with time, don't wait for it to catch-up with you first, it is therefore better for you to do thing differently than the former mentally oppressed generation, you are free, be warned, the price to pay for letting time to catch-up with you first is too huge to pay. Believe me chances are, you may not afford it. The method to take, the method working better, is to act as if the original only exist because is kept on the picture by the force generated daily and motivating you that something is not visible, and need to be made visible. Such thoughts will keep you younger in every aspect of challenges you need to find the solution for.

5. LANGUAGE AS A TOOL

"If and African has no culture of reading,
then let him have the broader church teaching
him the ways to yearn to become to the terms of
being himself, for the transformation of the mental
environment to be created."

Chele Mthembu

Words communicated in a mode and context of artistic, artistic channeled to such extend that has the weight to revolutionize the one's self image.

The self image through language can be masterminded through the ability to differentiate, between the words carrying the ingredients rich enough to take a person from one point to the other.

For our existence as an individual and the society in general, to be protected and our interest to be advocated, it is only by investing time and efforts, in mastering the negotiation skills. Through such skills, we then need to openly repeatedly argue our point. The world of globalization has been developed to be capable of communicating the massage across, which put the interest of other nations at the fore front of the art of words. The capitalist, advocating his interests, he then took the advantage and, in the process he managed to assassinate the image of those who were targeted on that fishing program devised by the capitalist himself.

Language, as useful as it is the art of advocating the massage across, it has authorized the enrichment of those who have used it well centauries ago. It was through the use of it that Africans has ended up losing there identities, which translate to self image. Over and over they were told how their ways of living were out dated. With words, the creator God, can either build or bring about destruction. That can not be questioned. The society, especially in African countries, pays more attention on their mother tongue being the medium of instruction, they are more concerned about the protection of the language its self and the history of their heroes. There is nothing wrong about the fact that language is taught in educational institutions.

But language is one of the most powerful tool that need to be made the weapon of mass destruction, to destabilize the wall and the injustice that has been committed on the mind and the soul of the living human being, by the former slave master, the self-enriched capitalist and the former rulers of colonist powers.

The criminal activity, the offence made possible to be believed by the law maker, to be the true common ground, a way of living, was master-minded in such a way that, there must be no justice court of law in the entire global world, capable of ratifying such crime.

It is by the above argument that I will be basing my definition of language as 'the last resort, and the tool powered by the spoken words', needed for the ratification of mental refocusing for the real means of under-taking life journey.

Africans need to go on the struggle of using the language as the new model that have what it takes to pioneer an 'artistic spoken words'. The artistic spoken words has to define what and African are, and what they yearn to become.

And African, for the benefit of his future generation and for the sake of Africa needs as a continent, to yearn to define himself in his own terms. This is one of the struggles to be formulated, to ride until this definition is well embedded in the mind of those who are living the life, of being made the dolls that are positioned to be taken advantage. The time has come to revise thing as they used to be. We cannot fall for the idea of just remaining the same, we need to become 'the used to be', and we need to pass-over the boundaries, to become new human being transformed while keeping the base the same.

A 'new bible of the artistic spoken words' calls on the recruit for politicians, academics and the artists in general, to join on the formation of this formula. The base has been formulated by the late black ancestor. People like Steve Biko, Macurce Guervy, Murtin Luther King JN and Mulcom X, to name few. They have already given up the base of the formulae. All that we need is making the formation and strengthening of the strategy that will enhance the spreading of the message. These must be strategic that won't just be spreading the content of the country's historical legacy, but a way of life. If and African has no culture of reading, then let him have the broader church teaching him the ways to yearn to become to the terms of being himself, for the transformation of the mind environment to be created.

6. OPPRESSION FOR POINT OF REFERENCE

"The play-field of gaining the authority over others starts by convincing them, and reasoning beyond their capability of thinking."

Chele Mthembu

One day when Jesus was on the temple, teaching the people and preaching the good news, the chief priest, and the teachers of the law, together with the elders. Came and sad to him, 'tell as on what right do you have to do these things? Who gave you this right?'

Jesus answered them, "now let me ask you a question, tell me, did John's right to peptize come from the God or from the man? They then started to argue among themselves. What shall we say? If we say 'from God' he will say then why then did you not believe John. "But if we say from man, this whole crowd here will stone us; because they are convinced that John was a prophet. We don't know where it comes from". They answered. And Jesus said to them, "Nether will I tell you, then, by what right I do these things".

The play-field of gaining the authority over others starts by convincing them, and reasoning beyond their capability of thinking. Through making the play field to seems much conducive for the kingdom that they thought they will gain paradise of it some day, whereas they will never set their feet onto that kingdom, the kingdom that doesn't even exist

7. NOMINATING A PATH, THUG LIFE

". . . . each gap found and practiced with passion,
is the remedy for preventing health hazards,
for those who are practicing it with such
required passion"

Chele Mthembu

In its interpretation, it is the liberation of choice. God knew about it, and he could not leave it behind on his creation. The gap seekers in the world of gaps, found it, they are the thugs. Should we blame them for their life style? Hell no, it's a liberation of nominating a path to follow in life. This point can not be argued any father than this, because it is the reality not to be negated. Negating it is removing a gap in life, and at the same time, creating the very same gap of the same magnitude. That's pointless efforts. Any way, if God new what he was doing, if we human remove the element of balance, do we have another element of our own to balance life, I don't think so.

Those who are seeking the gap to provided by life, commit no sin, no matter what kind of gap they find on their journey, if ever that gap can be analyzed, it will associate with some feeling and emotional satisfaction, in so doing, healing at the times it is practice. The point here is that, each gap found and practiced with passion, is the remedy for preventing health hazards, for those who are practicing it with such required passion. Let's leave different individual to fill gaps of their own choice, in doing so, that will also prevent the over saturation of majority gap subscriber, which will imbalance life.

8. INSTITUTE OF CHOICE

"Act as if, wrong was supposed to happen in order for
you to have, some kind of new life solutions."

Chele Mthembu

The road travelled by the common human, can lead to free production of thoughts. The reason he can not come near to this point is the fact that, for his existence to be known, he take the initiative to travel the path leading to its point known as cross-road. When he gets there, this person will seek a way to follow. Should all the diverging three direction reject him due to the regulations, a common man then will remember the hiding shadow stating that, the cross of Jesus will free you, but only when you give your life to him.

Life is the greatest opponents of a person existence. To be efficient against it one need to walk the tight rope, and still maintain the balance. But how can you maintain the balance if you are giving you life to fantasy, when rejection spread like a communicable disease, you run to the hiding place provided by religion.

Walking the tight rope against life requires the following:

- Remaining calm as if nothing is happening;
- Wasting no time and energy on complaining;
- Going through point wrong to point right, as if, wrong have no effects of the out-come in life. Act as if, wrong was supposed to happen in order for you to have some kind of new life solutions. Any way it was bound to happen, it is life and we have no control over it, but control and manage its out-comes;

- But realistically speaking, you need to have a degree of set point, which will help you to pause the going for a while. This usually takes place to prevent the efforts that are not conducive even if taken well. You can not plant a seed that need summer weather on winter season and expect the productive efforts.

- What differentiate the quieter from the winners is the fact that quieter when arriving at the pausing state of mind during the set point, their mind loses the triggering point. But a winner, do have and maintain the mode of triggering, by remaining calm and listening to the leading sounds of nothing that requires sounds of something. That different sounds, has a line of direction that needs to be analyzed for the purpose of finding the triggering mode. Be the winner; maintain the mode of nothing leading to something.

- Whatever the choice you have made, either bad or good, makes you the institute of choice. Look for ways directing you to nothing, because there is treasure in the direction of nothing. This is due to the fact that, once you enter into nothing, nothing becomes something, depending on what you do in such condition you find yourself onto. Your problems and your efforts that are amounting to nothing at present, such problems at their own, are basically your raw material to amount to treasure when time goes-by.

9. ZONE OF REJECTIONS, FOR PROSPERITY

"It is good for the human being to reject the feeling of becoming constant"

Chele Mthembu

The deference between the zones lies onto, the comfort that we get out of what we know against what we fear to be there but not known. Hence, fighting to stay at all times at the comfort zones; never provide the living being with a long term healing process. It is good for the human being to reject the feeling of becoming constant, with the feeling of getting to know what is there behind what the eye can not see.

10. ADVOCATING FOR TANGIBILITY

". . . I recognize my surface through its character.
I reject to be submissive to rough surface if I'm
smooth surfaced, I also reject to be submissive to,
smooth surface, if I'm surfaced the other way,
doing that, I'm maintaining my character."

Chele Mthembu

As it means able to touch, so, have you ever gave a thought on who you really advocate for? Are you advocating for your own tangibility? Tell you what, myself I wrote this book with a mission of advocating for my tangible to be noticed both, spiritually and materially. For this, I reject to be meditating on the tangible of other things, before meditating on my own existence one's first.

I advocate on tangibility of my own based on the need to know the texture of my own surface, then through that, the texture of other thing will be made known to me, since well the smoothness and roughness of external object and character of others, are not necessary know on their own, but through how knowledgeable I recognize my surface through its character. I reject to be submissive to rough surface if I'm smooth surfaced, I also reject to be submissive to, smooth surface, if I'm surfaced the other way, doing that, I'm maintaining my character. If you have given your mind for the master of colonization and you refuse to let go of it, that's fine. But for me and those who are willing to give it a try, how about we subscribe on meditating on self made surfaced character, allowing for self advocacy. Through that we can proudly testify on the domination authorized by self advocacy, because our advocacy is tangible. Do not compromise your self worth; speak on your behalf if ever the call to do so arises. But above all, free yourself, speak your mind, your world of interest can only be defendant by you because you know it better than others.

11. TESTIFYING BASED ON REALITY, NOT FANTASY

"Nothing; can only be available if ever, that very nothing testify on its own availability, not basing its availability onto the availability of something."

Chele Mthembu

A human species can not testify about the truth as if they are separated from the truth it's self. In other words, truth about the existence of something can only be correctly testified by the maker of the object, a fact or opinion. It is therefore not accurate for the man to testify even by the greatness of nature, because nature is the only force that does knows the real truth beyond a human species. By this I mean, God is the supper power, but, testifying that the control of our achievement and our lives is within the palm of his hand, is not the accurate conclusion.

The existence of who we are is based solely onto how much we believe in us. We fantasize about the universe being in control of our mental freedom, and in so doing we are quick to degrade the authority we do have over things. The reality is that without us there is nothing to exist. Nothing; can only be available if ever, that very nothing testify on its own availability, not basing its availability onto the availability of something. The same, something can be available only when that something itself, testify on its availability, not basing its availability onto the availability of nothing. None of the two can degrade itself on giving the other one authority over its expenses. Hence we the authorize species, should not degrade ourselves worth, we are the reality to be testified up-on, done so not by others but by ourselves. I am therefore who I work to achieve

12. INJECTION OF NEW IDEAS

"A human being is the idea on his own.
Idealize yourself; take you presence as the application
to be tested at a daily basis"

Chele Mthembu

The fun of ideas do fade away if they usually come from one side or same source at all times in a team. The intellectuals, the academics and different leaders, make the equations, daily functioning is implemented by the common people. Occasionally, these people, professionals, need to make the deal with the common people as they take their sit in generating the ideas.

You will be surprised how this common people can work out the equation from the answer found on using that given available equation. They can break the equation to its components. The interesting part of it is that, they will break such components to new groups of different series.

Those groups of series can then be taken by the academics and other leader, to device new application. In so doing, the world which is inclusive and leading to commonality can be created, whereby no man is better than the other one. Injection of new ideas can not be categorized, come with your own set and work through it. But for the benefit of different species, let your set be inclusive. A human being is the idea on his own. Idealize yourself; take you presence as the application to be tested at a daily basis. Break what you've got; it can be thoughts, money, time, and all the identified parts of life needing your attention, into number of series of new events, at the end of the year, then device a new application of who you are, at the beginning of the year through to the end. Be inclusive to yourself first, before you become inclusive to other. No one is here to make you the specialist of how to live life. You are a brand; despite the qualifications you've got. Brand yourself.

13. OPTIMIZATION MOVEMENT

". . . success on its own has no ending, because
when it does end, without looking for redirection,
then it has never been a success to begin with"

Chele Mthembu

The optimization of the mind capacity can only be achieved when the definitions of life forces are redefined, and their scripture kept remaining the same. It is therefore the movement of passion, which handles errors as the mechanism necessary to destabilizing the environment. Perfection attained through the usual route for many years hinder the capacity to get the new shape of development. Hence according to my definition of success, I will say, success on its own has no ending, because when it does end, without looking for redirection, then it has never been a success to begin with.

Repeated redirections, is the movement of optimization for the daily expansion of the mental capacity. Growth in life is expanded by how one handles life errors.

14. NEEDS OF THE SPIRITS

"To attain high standard of life,
it is therefore recommended to give the
soul its Godly created needs"

Chele Mthembu

Soul that has been provided for with its needs, form the structure considered to near perfectionism. Even after any kind of straining. The death tissues of the wound can be repaired by inflicting more pain on the physical body. This is done by removing the very same death tissues. The needle has to go through the skin to cause more of a pain, but in the hospital settings, the use of drugs makes the pain to go away. The process will then go on as if the is nothing happening.

If the above can be achievable, imagine what can happen if the soul of the man get away with its natural needs. To attain high standard of life, it is therefore recommended to give the soul its Godly created needs. Both spiritual and physically, the soul should be hungry and thirsty for the wave of any kind to move one from the direction of known to the diverging directions of the unknown.

Decolonization of the mind is beyond reasonable doubt, the movement of passion, from the known to the unknown given sport of zones. Therefore, the spirit is said to be enough, not hungry, not thirsty, if and only if, the person has in life practiced and experienced by himself any out-come onto his set point in a particular task. If ever one has not done so him self, the thought of others and the knowledge can not serve as his needs for his soul, when it reaches the point of tearing-up.

Physical pain needs drug, but the broken soul with thirsty spirit needs a wave of motion from to reach the unknown zone. It needs to adjust to this zone first, only after then will it heals. As I have said about zones, fighting to stay at all times at the comfort zones never provide the living being with a long term healing process

It is by this theory putted into practice, that, we can therefore make a claim that recalls known zone to be replaced with the zone of unknown, which is the decolonization of the mind. This can be achieved through a wave of any kind of motion to the direction that does not matter at all. As long as, is not the zone designed by the mind bankers in relation to behavior, with the intention to bankrupts a human being soul. In all fields of life, no matter how things have been taken from you, bankrupt is to be regarded as the investment of more return to come your ways, due to more having been taken away from you the same as capital can be taken from you to be invested, and produce capital growth on interest point of view. All it takes it's just a change of behavior on how you view failure and losses coming your ways.

THE DELEGATED ATTENTION

"Curiosity, it's a chained events, a way of life,
it is life at its own definition"

Chele Mthembu

It happens to be the modified crafted piece of work that is not narrowed by the limited resource that have crafted it, but by the delegated attention that has being paid-up during the cutting period.

For some time, I was bored by the fact that, my tertiary education did not amount to anything. And that I am a drop-out. I then took a pen and a paper, the idea was to define the real reason why things turn to be the opposite of the master plan. It was quite difficult not having a clear angle to write about. One thing for sure that I only knew, was that I have to write, based on the redefinition of turning things differently. I need to know what is behind the opposite. I then delegated my attention driven by the power contained on the feelings of curiosity.

The delegated attention, on it's center having embedded by the curiosity instinct, the curiosity instinct vibrating like the powerful magnetic field between two magnet, gave me the angel in life that need to be redefined.

On the process I also found out that, my self too, I need to be redefined. I had I stigma, a stigma of being a drop out, with no experience to back-up my job hunting. Above all, I was turning thirty yeas of age.

Both of my parents having past away, none of the relatives even bothering to give a helping hand, brothers having found their way of disappearing on the space.

Curiosity took the center of thoughts in my life. I had to make up for the lost time, and the capital that should have come-up with that very same time. My miserable life, redefined on a paper with the help of a black pen, was the weapon, to be utilized for recovering the lost branding mechanism of my character, oh no, I had a character by that time. Remember life hardships build a stronger character. I needed to attach material on it for its smooth transitional period from the age of thirty to period of my life destiny.

Let me take you through, just to give you the picture of the emotional and the mental game strengths, which can be embedded by becoming curiously and courageously accepting changes brought by it through self awareness. Curiosity with courage put you on the spot light of becoming the leading, profitable entity as a man. Curiosity, it is a chained events, a way of life; it is life at its own definition.

People whom are on their daily basis delegating their attention on practicing this chain, way of life, generally they are creating the master piece in which they are the main leading actors of the craft its self. Everywhere, in which the delegated attention is not producing profitable means, translate to the fact that, curiosity on its center is not really producing the intensified magnetic field. Its center is then presumed to be death, presumed to be impaired. It is therefore in need of the right stimulus.

There are some few psychological factors that we have to go through them in order to get to the right stimulus. We are about to turn over the pages, what are they? Well, go through the next pages to find out.

1. THE PSYCHOLOGICAL WAR, REGULAR PATTERN

". . . . the produced results in most cases, lack the spiritual satisfaction, if ever, the family as a unit was neglected during the process of such results attainment."

Chele Mthembu

THE GRAVITY OF TRUTH

In a practical aspect, regular pattern is a way in which focusing as a tool is much desired to be putted into consideration. A person whom is practicing the regularity, is presumed the one with lesser or even have none stimulus at all. In reality; eating one plate of meal day-in and day-out, doesn't do any good for the body. The taste will fade away, no matter how great is the plate.

In this exercise of the relationship, I will be taking you through the process of "interruption of the soul, body and mind kind of environment". It consists of six interruptions of mental war.

The number one, being the psychological war, the regular factor, this one regulate the entire other field of mental war.

Now here are you, in the world of thinking and disturbance is not welcomed on the process. Your child is in need of your attention and you made it clear that no disturbance. Your lover needs to steal five minute of your time but you are court-up on your daily routine.

The best thing about the tool of focusing is that, it produces results. The worst thing about it is that as much as the regular pattern is involved, the produced results in most cases, lack the spiritual satisfaction, if ever, the family as a unit was neglected during the process of such results attainment. Family wants to be contributing to the success of every individual forming its part. Psychological war, regularities, simply damages the spiritual satisfaction. It also has the power to hinder the clearance of the mental muddy of tress. Failure to clear-up this mental muddiness, prevent the future legacy of looking back and smiling together with a family concerning the 'moments of interruptions they have created in the process that leaded one to goal attainment.

At the work place, let the employees have a minutes meeting with you without having to make appointment for fitting onto your regular routine. Make some means as the manager to fade away the regular pattern and you will psychologically improve the work place mental health. This period can be allowed for the purpose of recharging. This means that, the regularity can be practiced for a month or so, then, when we introduce the next field of war based on the psychological factor, this one has to fade away. For that matter, how about we introduce the next.

2. PSYCHOLOGICAL WAR, FAMILY INCORPORATED

"As much as the criminals are ruling and determining our safety, when dealing with them, teach a child to go extremely on self defense"

Chele Mthembu

This is the team work leaded by the parents. It has to do with the defiance mechanism at all cost for the needed life survival. For the belonging structure, parents need to be making time for playing with their children. Include them in the making of critical decision making.

The family incorporated has to do with the following; the responding mechanism that a child has be tough of, for the defense of his own individualism and protection of upholding the name, pride and the future existence of the family legacy.

In this game, the fighting tools have to vary, from the slightly one to more drastically one. But the entire different varying tools are the single one's that forms the family observational skills.

Method of observational skills is the chain of regular events. Here the child get used to the regularity, once something imposes on these pattern, it will react as the stimuli, it will then be regarded by the child as something in need of drastically, or slightly to be taken care off.

Since well you have taught the child the responding mechanism, if ever there is a need for self-deface, the child won't hesitate to respond accordingly. No one on his or her up-bringing should be denied the physical responding mechanism, and the limitation to extend which it should end. As much as the criminals are ruling and determining our safety, when dealing with them, teach a child to go extremely on self defense, in this instance, violence is more encourage. The moral teaching of turning the face to be beaten on the next cheek is not an option any more. That moral practice ended with the era of Jesus Christ.

During my teen age, I was bullied emotionally, whereby the guy will just have the courage to split on my face. What I then did was to wipe my face, without any respond. On the other hand, one picked up a fight with me; I excused my self, for what because I got a hit on the back of my shoulder when I was not even looking. The boy took a rock, throwing it on my back; running did not help me with a thing. I was a coward injured for not facing a challenge on self defense for the survival of my own safety, even though God gave me the right to do so.

The moral value of being non-violently took over my feeling, my emotions was suppressed and not allowing me to act accordingly. It is basically not my father whom taught me these pathetic responding values. On two occasions, I have seen my father in action responding violently. He was not a man for starting a street fight, but when the need came-up; he mostly preferred to beat first. He did so based on the fact that he did not start the fight, his not even interested on it, so what his delegated attention was all about on this issue, basically was to end the fight as soon as possible.

Hence he beating fight at all times. The difference between my father and me, in relations to self defense is that, I became the victim of something I did not start, my father never allowed such nonsense in his life.

After fifteen years, it was then that I have recognized the need for facing challenges hand on.

Then subscribing to my father's method of responding becomes the need for me.

Bit first and biting harder at any situation, especially on something interfering with my interest, became the practice that I under took for survival.

The psychological war, family incorporated, pay attention on ending the unfavorable situation, imposed by life to one's chain of events. Hence the urgent need of responding in order for the delegated attention to be able to create the favorable situation; which capacitate to accumulation of survival method. Parents need to teach the child to capacitate to accumulation of survival methods. Also from young age, children should be equipped with the skills to choose quality lover. Lovers are not chosen on what material they are already in passion of, but by what character and legacy can they bring to the family. Having no material, but possessing the will and the vision to attain wealth, is the most important qualities to be looked for when a lover is identified and be brought to form a family team.

3. EXCUSE NOT TOLERATED, PSYCHOLOGICAL WAR FOR CHILDREN

"The morality for forgiveness in true reasoning and in facts: expose the forgiver to take consequences of other people's actions, and on the later stage, the forgiven one capitalizing on the forgiver's sweat".

Chele Mthembu

On the presence of growing up with two parents, and the first one is at all times making some excuses and the second parent has room big enough to accommodate such excuses, then, the child is exposed to two choices to make his drive for survival from. His therefore become an excuse maker or create a room big enough to tolerate excuses, either in the name of love or respect. If one does not make one choice from the two; then he turn to take both behavior practiced by parents.

If the other parent can only tolerate the excuses that were beyond the excuse maker, then the child has the third option.

The three choice delegated attentions for excuse incorporated environment, prepares the child for the consequence of future failure omitting what his supposed to be doing in thinking that excuses will be tolerated.

I have a nephew at home. After the age of eighteen, the biological father showed up. The time that my sister was pregnant this man was not beside her. The child was born and the father's family was told, but they never showed up. It was said that this man refuse the responsibility, above all, deny ever impregnating my sister.

His argument after such a long time was that, he was young and stupid. I took that as an excuse based on the fact that for years he claimed to have been young, I was very younger than him, and I played the role of father figure, even though I was ten years younger than he was. I did not even have a child by that period.

What need to be done was therefore done; I refused to take his argument for he thought he can benefit just like that from his past failures. I refused to make a fool of my self due to my compassion. He asked for forgiveness, I couldn't give him any because I have never had hard feelings for him. Excuses was not tolerated, he failed to give my nephew identity, what kind of identity will he ever give at nineteen years. I guess it's only a destruction of what I have already constructed.

The moral teaching will take argument side of forgiving others for their sin, in most instances; the very same moral is used for the benefit of the one whom did not sweat on the constructions of a product maturing process.

The morality for forgiveness in true reasoning and in facts expose the forgiver to take consequences of other people's actions, and on the later stage, the forgiven one capitalizing on the forgiver's sweat.

The father's family failed to teach their child at an early age that, one need to take on the skills of bending the wood while still wet and soft. Therefore the whole principle of psychological war, excuse not tolerated is based on the fact of, never wait for the child to show beard before starting the process of future preparation. The earlier you teach the child that, the sooner is he capacitating on the art of, self engagement on fishing for his destiny calling in life. Parents, teach responsibility.

4. PSYCHOLOGICAL WAR, ASKING FOR FAVORS

"This habit may be the major power factor on the mind of a female. It is not a problem if it is benefiting her in any way"

Chele Mthembu

Practicing on the mode of asking for favors are in most cases indebted to other at all times. The behavior that is practiced by majority of our female, are generally on the drive of relaying on the favors from the man's side. Woman turn to ask for anything, it could be lunch, free lift to bigger things. Not like it's wrong to do that, but the thing is on the presence of children, it is something else, especially if that it is done on the impression of "I am a woman and what ever that I ask, will be provided for in the name of my feminism". This habit may be the major power factor on the mind of a female. It is not a problem if it is benefiting her in any way. The practice doesn't have to be transmitted as an electric voltage or current to charge children in order to behave in that manner also.

A relationship which has started over such favors, survives for a time being. It was only allowed by the man during the state of reliving the emotional tension. Once the tension is relived, the mistrust takes over; the mistrust is basically stimulated by the manner in which the two have met. A man sees a woman now as an opportunist whom can go for any man as long as such a man can provide favors of some sort.

It is therefore best for a mother to provide the leadership direction for children. Rather than asking for favors at all times, in other occasions, provide favors for people of different gender. This will let the girl child to avoid the trap of being taken advantage of by men on her thinking that she's powerful, based on her gender, whereas she is just the opposite of that. A woman whom clearly act capably and also showing the gentle side of feminism, gets more chances of sustaining a long term relationship with any man of sober mind.

The boy on the other hand, having grew-up on this situation of a mother challenging, and rejecting some favors at some times, won't be subjected to raise-up children whom their father have deserted them. He may not do so, whereas, his own children are dying of hunger and craving for their father's love and guidance. This principle defines that a woman can be able to fit on man's shoes if ever she plays her card carefully in rising-up children. Children are the legacy we believe, will drive our future as time goes by. Desire therefore to shaped their direction indirectly so, as they will have to shape themselves directly through their efforts.

5. PSYCHOLOGICAL WAR, RATING FACTOR

"I try to learn from the past,
but I plan for the future by focusing exclusively
on the present. That's were the fun is."

The man went on by saying;

"I wasn't satisfied just to earn a good living. I was
looking to make a statement".

By Donald Trump, Quotes

The psychological war, rating factor, is the exclusiveness of the present lived on the foundation of the past. In this context, I will like to define it as, a factor to be applied as a neutralizing one, in the beginning, the middle and the end of the year strategy. It's a self rating storage for the planning at the beginning of the year, in the middle, it just checks on the progress made on six months period, and re-examine the plan on that moment of the present. The end of the factor is entirely based on the statement rating the efforts made. That's were the quote "I wasn't satisfied just to earn a good living. I was looking to make a statement" come into practice.

During the state of confusion, not knowing what decision to be taken, the brain of the human being is therefore in the process of receiving its sharpness. When the process is done, that's were the fun is.

Never fear the state of not knowing the right direction to follow; either one you take has the fun part of it.

If you take the opposite one which does not bring the desired product development you planned for, it is then store it for the next project.

It is therefore not advisable to throw out the opposite unsuccessful plan to the dust bin; it may come useful in the next project. Not all project are made successful by following the direct working strategy, some are successful on, the in-direct deals.

The above can be achieved with the right mind exercised on the state of taking calculated risk when prepared to deal with the consequence of your action at a later stage, and having the fun of doing what needed to be done now.

6. PSYCHOLOGICAL WAR, ADAPTING TO THE SITUATION. BEHIND FEAR AND FAILURE

The main meaning behind fear is,

"Focus for entrance, authorizing results".

Chele Mthembu

A man with the right knowledge and the understanding of the behavior of the reptile can device his own capability to with-stand daily challenges:

"Lizards are cold-blooded and begin the day with a body temperature that is too low for much activity, and they must bask in the sun to increase their body temperature. While basking in the sun they stand sideways to it and flatten and tilt their bodies to maximize heat intake. They can also spread their bodies and change their skin color from light to dark to increase heat intake. However, in hot desert areas lizards run the risk of overheating and have also developed ways of losing heat."

Let as therefore take on the interpretation of this in relation to the human behavior, and once again borrowing on the quotes from

Donald Trump when he said, "Experience taught me a few things. One is to listen to your gut, no matter how good something sounds on paper. The second is that you're generally better off sticking with what you know. And the third is that sometimes your best investments are the ones you don't make".

My take on this is that, fear of making a move out side the field that you normally operate within, can be beneficial at some point. But listening to your guts for not taking chances, at all times when fearing, when the impossibility get in your way, will leave you with no experience. Further more, it will also results in poverty due to failure to consider, and take advantage of the ingredients contained in the feelings of fear, as the best investment life is offering to you is hidden there.

Fear is the feelings that have been imbedded in a human being reaction in relation to the given point. As much as the Lizard is capable of basking in the sun, standing sideways to it and flatten and tilting their bodies to maximize heat intake, it is what we also need to do for coping with fear. Lizards are cold-blooded and begin the day with a body temperature that is too low for much activity, but even if they have to do this daily, they stick to what is working for them, as much as it has been said about experience teaching one to stick to what one know best.

Fear together with negative energy that comes along with it, it's a weapon to be used at a given point. It was prepared for as, so that we can take advantage of it when faced with quick decision to be made. We need to use what we've got, no matter what are the circumstances, just like in hot desert area lizards running the risk of overheating, we have to use fear as a weapon of quick action, although we may run the rick of regretting our action at a later stage.

We will come up with the mechanism of getting things right later, the same way the Lizard have also developed ways of losing heat in hot desert areas.

The main meaning behind fear is,
"Focus for entrance, authorizing results.

A person with a great focus has a clear vision and efforts which is directed to certain attainment. For such efforts or inputs to reach their destination, the must be an entrance.

Once focus has penetrated on its entrance; it becomes the dominating factor whereby it authorizes desired or the expected out comes.

The entrance determines the roughness or smoothness of the out come results. Although this entrance may be not bigger enough to capacitate the focus, let as maintain its needs of both physical and chemical requirements. In so doing, what ever the input produce as the output will be beneficial to the action taker.

Psychological war, adapting to the situation behind fear and failure, is nothing else but traveling of the road without having influenced by its roughness, neither by its smoothness.

Remember the good about the roughness of your problem is that it produces the mental and the physical picture of its own kind. That is going to make you the newer rated version of a man, or a woman of her own kind.

The rough entrance is the science of new development, unlike the smooth one in which same known products are obtainable. For which entrance you will take at all times, it entirely depends on you.

INTEGRATED FIGHT OF LIFE, IS FAITH

"Do not expose your intention publicly before you have
examined the majestic power of such intentions first"

Chele Mthembu

The fight of life is basically integrated within you. It is similarly having the characteristics of the heart. The acting bond between none existing and the existing potion of life is tightly put into place by the mechanism of faith.

The heart is protected in the thoracic cavity and has to support the circulation of blood to the whole body. It is enclosed by the diaphragm, the sternum and both sided ribs. Similarly the faith has to be protected the same way the heart is.

Here are the two way faith protections:

1. Do not expose your intention publicly before you have examined the majestic power of such intention first.

Patience is the factor protection. God as the majestic creator, he had patience on creating a human being. In so doing made the cover up of his intention. He first created other thing, and then followed his majestic plan, a human being. Faith need to practice on the basics of first thing first principles, even God himself knew that. He had his intentions exposed after full elimination of his picture of the world and everything onto it.

The process of the world picture was therefore not risked by God in making a man into his image first, and then had the majestic thought revealed to him. If ever God could have tried such risk, man could have taken the plan from God and acted like God himself.

2. Factor two, protection of faith exclude the feelings of courage, for the goal having been virtualized.

The heart works hand in hand with the lung in the thoracic cavity, but it takes the network of arteries and veins to make the complete circulation in the system. If a smaller vein is leaking, the entire system is considered to be at risk. From that, we can abstract the fact that, to get ahead in life, it is not God only painting the way forward, your efforts is more important than any other high power. Be in power as much as the vain in the body, serve your potion in the bigger picture.

Make your presence felt, make sure that you are respected for the fact that if you become neglected, the rest of the system collapses.

For every task you under-take, negotiate bearing in mind that, you are the power not to be neglected.

"As a human being,
I'm God,
Therefore, I'm acting like him"

Hence, I'm the power making the future to exist.Nam tem ipienterfera nerum ium tum tuitius postre ce mant.